THROUGH ELIZABETHAN EYES

CAMBRIDGE
UNIVERSITY PRESS
LONDON: BENTLEY HOUSE
NEW YORK, TORONTO, BOMBAY
CALCUTTA, MADRAS: MACMILLAN
TOKYO: MARUZEN COMPANY LTD

THROUGH ELIZABETHAN EYES

AN ABRIDGMENT OF
LIFE IN SHAKESPEARE'S ENGLAND
FOR JUNIOR READERS

By

J. DOVER WILSON
C.H., Litt.D., F.B.A.

Professor of Rhetoric and English Literature in the University of Edinburgh; Hon. Fellow of Gonville and Caius College, Cambridge

CAMBRIDGE
AT THE UNIVERSITY PRESS
1939

PRINTED IN GREAT BRITAIN

CONTENTS

ILLUSTRATIONS

PREFACE

This book, an abridgment of my *Life in Shakespeare's England*, is intended for junior readers. Nearly all the extracts have been taken from books and pamphlets written between 1564 and 1616, the dates of Shakespeare's birth and death. The spelling has been modernized and a glossary added to explain old-fashioned words, or words that look modern but had a different meaning in the days when Shakespeare lived.

J. D. W.

April 1939

I

ENGLAND AND THE ENGLISH

SHAKESPEARE was born in 1564, six years after Queen Elizabeth's accession to the throne, and died in 1616, nine years before that of Charles I. This book will give you an idea of what life was like in England during this period and it will do so in the words partly of Shakespeare himself and partly of other men actually living in the period, men whom Shakespeare might have seen, who knew at first hand the England he knew.

Let us begin by quoting Shakespeare's praise of England, praise which he puts into the mouth of his dying John of Gaunt; and then take a look at the English people of the time through the eyes of two foreigners, a German and a Dutchman, who visited England in 1598 and 1575 respectively.

This royal throne of kings, this scepter'd isle,
This earth of majesty, this seat of Mars,
This other Eden, demi-paradise,
This fortress built by Nature for herself
Against infection and the hand of war,
This happy breed of men, this little world,
This precious stone set in the silver sea,
Which serves it in the office of a wall,
Or as a moat defensive to a house,
Against the envy of less happier lands,
This blessed plot, this earth, this realm, this England....

Richard II, II. i. 40–50

The English

The English are grave like the Germans, lovers of shew; followed wherever they go by whole troops of servants, who wear their masters' arms in silver fastened to their left arms, and are not undeservedly ridiculed for wearing tails hanging down their backs. They excel in dancing and music, for they are active and lively, though of a thicker make than the French; they cut their hair close on the middle of the head, letting it grow on either side; they are good sailors, and better pirates, cunning, treacherous, and thievish; above 300 are said to be hanged annually at London. Beheading with them is less infamous than hanging. They give the wall as the place of honour. Hawking is the common sport of the gentry. They are more polite in eating than the French, consuming less bread, but more meat, which they roast in perfection. They put a great deal of sugar in their drink. Their beds are covered with tapestry, even those of farmers. They are often molested with the scurvy, said to have first crept into England with the Norman conquest. Their houses are commonly of two stories, except in London, where they are of three and four, though but seldom of four; they are built of wood; those of the richer sort with bricks; their roofs are low, and where the owner has money, covered with lead. They are powerful in the field, successful against their enemies, impatient of anything like slavery; vastly fond of great noises that fill the ear, such as the firing of cannon, drums, and the ringing of bells, so that in London it is common for a number of them, that have got a glass [of ale] in their heads, to go up into some belfry, and ring the bells for hours together, for the sake of exercise. If they see a foreigner, very well made or particularly handsome, they will say, "It is a pity he is not an Englishman".

PAUL HENTZNER, *Travels in England*, 1598 [Rye]

English women

Wives in England . . . are not kept so strictly as they are in Spain or elsewhere. Nor are they shut up: but they have the free management of the house or housekeeping, after the fashion of those of the Netherlands, and others their neighbours. They go to market to buy what they like best to eat. They are well dressed, fond of taking it easy, and commonly leave the care of household matters and drudgery to their servants. They sit before their doors, decked out in fine clothes, in order to see and be seen by the passers-by. In all banquets and feasts they are shown the greatest honour; they are placed at the upper end of the table, where they are the first served; at the lower end they help the men. All the rest of their time they employ in walking and riding, in playing at cards or otherwise, in visiting their friends and keeping company, conversing with their equals (whom they term gossips) and their neighbours, and making merry with them at child-births, christenings, churchings and funerals; and all this with the permission and knowledge of their husbands, as such is the custom. Although the husbands often recommend to them the pains, industry and care of the German or Dutch women, who do what the men ought to do both in the house and in the shops, for which services in England men are employed, nevertheless the women usually persist in retaining their customs. This is why England is called the Paradise of married women. The girls who are not yet married are kept much more rigorously and strictly than in the Low Countries.

The women are beautiful, fair, well-dressed and modest, which is seen there more than elsewhere, as they go about the streets without any covering either of huke or mantle, hood, veil, or the like. Married women only, wear a hat both in the street and in the house; those unmarried go without a hat, although ladies of distinction have lately learnt to cover their faces with silken masks or vizards, and feathers,—for indeed they change very easily, and that every year, to the astonishment of many.

VAN METEREN, *Nederlandtsche Historie*, 1575 [Rye]

II

CHILDHOOD IN THE COUNTRY

SHAKESPEARE grew up in the little country town of Stratford-on-Avon. He was the son of a farmer and wool-dealer, John Shakespeare, one of the principal men of the town; and he probably attended the grammar school, where a free education was provided for the sons of all citizens of Stratford, and where he would learn to read Latin. He learnt much too from the river and the woods and the meadows which surrounded his home, while it is clear that someone, his mother or his nurse, told him stories of the fairies and uncanny spirits which almost every one at that time believed might be seen. In Shakespeare's plays the country is never very far away. *A Midsummer Night's Dream*, *As You Like It* and *The Winter's Tale* are especially full of country scenes and country people; in *The Merry Wives of Windsor* we have a picture of life at Windsor which must have been very much like that of life at Stratford; and in 2 *Henry IV* Master Justice Shallow and Master Justice Silence introduce us to country gentlemen.

§ 1. COUNTRY-FOLK

A fair and happy milkmaid

The queen of curds and cream.

The Winter's Tale, IV. iv. 161

A fair and happy milkmaid is a country wench, that is so far from making herself beautiful by art, that one look of hers is able to put all face-physic out of countenance. She knows a fair look is but a dumb orator to commend virtue, therefore minds it not. All her excellences stand in her so silently, as if they had stolen upon her without her knowledge. The lining of her apparel (which is herself) is far better than outsides of tissue: for though she be not arrayed in the spoil of the silkworm, she is decked in innocency, a far better wearing. She doth not, with lying long abed, spoil both her complexion and conditions. Nature hath taught her too immoderate sleep is rust to the soul. She rises therefore with chanticleer, her dame's cock, and at night makes the lamb her curfew. In milking a cow, and straining the teats through her fingers, it seems that so sweet a milk-press makes the milk the whiter or sweeter; for never came almond glove or aromatic ointment on her palm to taint it. The golden ears of corn fall and kiss her feet when she reaps them, as if they wished to be bound and led prisoners by the same hand that felled them. Her breath is her own, which scents all the year long of June, like a new-made hay-cock. She makes her hand hard with labour, and her heart soft with pity: and when winter evenings fall early (sitting at her merry wheel) she sings a defiance to the giddy wheel of fortune. She doth all things with so sweet a grace, it seems ignorance will not suffer her to do ill, being her mind is to do well. She bestows her year's wages at next fair; and in choosing her garments, counts no bravery in the world like decency. The garden and bee-hive are all her physic and chirurgery, and she lives the longer for it.

SIR THOMAS OVERBURY, *Characters*, 1614–16

I. *Where Shakespeare went to School*

A shepherd

Corin. Sir, I am a true labourer: I earn that I eat, get that I wear, owe no man hate, envy no man's happiness, glad of other men's good, content with my harm; and the greatest of my pride is to see my ewes graze and my lambs suck.

As You Like It, III. ii. 78–82

An honest shepherd is a man that well verifies the Latin piece, *qui bene latuit bene vixit*: he lives well that lives retired: for he is always thought the most innocent because he is least public: and certainly I cannot well resolve you whether his sheep or he be more innocent. Give him fat lambs and fair weather, and he knows no happiness beyond them. He shows, most fitly among all professions, that nature is contented with a little. For the sweet fountain is his fairest alehouse: the sunny bank his best chamber. Adam had never less need of neighbours' friendship; nor was at any time troubled with neighbours' envy less than he: the next grove or thicket will defend him from a shower: and if they be not so favourable, his homely palace is not far distant. He proves quietness to be best contentment, and that there is no quietness like a certain rest. His flock affords him his whole raiment, outside and linings, cloth and leather: and instead of much costly linen, his little garden yields hemp enough to make his lockram shirts: which do preserve his body sweetened against court-itch and poxes, as a cere-cloth sweetens carcasses. He gives the just epitome of a contented man: for he is neither daunted with lightning and thunder, nor overjoyed with spring-time and harvest. His daily life is a delightful work, whatsoever the work be; whether to mend his garments, cure a diseased sheep, instruct his dog, or change pastures: and these be pleasant actions, because voluntary, patient, not interrupted. . . . With little knowledge and a simple faith, he purifies his honest soul, in the same manner as he can wash his body in an obscure fountain better than in the wide ocean. When he seems lazy and void of action, I dare approve his harmless negligence, rather than many approved men's diligence. Briefly he is the perfect allegory of a most blessed governor: and he that will pursue the trope's invention, may make this character a volume.

JOHN STEPHENS, *Essayes and Characters*, 1615

§ 2. AMUSEMENT AND SPORT

Hunting

Come, shall we go and kill us venison?
And yet it irks me, the poor dappled fools,
Being native burghers of this desert city,
Should in their own confines with forked heads
Have their round haunches gor'd.

As You Like It, II. i. 21–25

I think it not amiss to begin and give that recreation precedency of place, which in mine opinion (however it may be esteemed partial) doth many degrees go before and precede all other, as being most royal for the stateliness thereof, most artificial for the wisdom and cunning thereof, and most manly and warlike for the use and endurance thereof. And this I hold to be the hunting of wild beasts in general: of which, as the chases are many, so will I speak of them particularly in their proper places.... But to proceed to my main purpose, you shall understand that as the chases are many which we daily hunt, as that of the stag, the buck, the roe, the hare, the fox, the badger, the otter, the boar, the goat and such like, so the pursuers or conquerors of these chases (speaking of hunting only) are but one kind of creatures, namely hounds.

GERVASE MARKHAM, *Countrey Contentments*, 1611

Preparations for the chase

Immediately after supper the huntsman should go to his master's chamber, and, if he serve a king, then let him go to the Master of the Games' chamber, to know his pleasure in what quarter he determineth to hunt the day following, that he may know his own quarter. That done, he may go to bed, to the end he may rise the earlier in the morning, according to the time and season, and according to the place where he must hunt. Then, when he is up and ready, let him drink a good draught and fetch his hound to make him break his fast a little. And let him not forget to fill his bottle with good wine. That done, let him take a little vinegar in the palm of his hand, and put it in the nostrils of his hound, for to make him snuff, to the end his scent may be the perfecter. Then let him to the wood. And if he chance by the way to find any hare, partridge, or any other beast or bird that is fearful, living upon seeds or pasturage, it is an evil sign or presage that he shall have but evil pastime that day. But if he find any beast of ravine, living upon prey, as wolf, fox, raven and such like, that is a token of good luck.

GEORGE TURBERVILE, *The noble arte of venerie or hunting*, 1576

The cry of the hounds

My hounds are bred out of the Spartan kind,
So flew'd, so sanded; and their heads are hung
With ears that sweep away the morning dew;
Crook-knee'd, and dew-lapp'd like Thessalian bulls;
Slow in pursuit, but match'd in mouth like bells,
Each under each.

A Midsummer Night's Dream, IV. i. 125–130

If you would have your kennel for sweetness of cry, then you must compound it of some large dogs that have deep solemn mouths and are swift in spending, which must, as it were, bear the bass in the consort, then a double number of roaring and loud ringing mouths which must bear the counter-tenor, then some hollow plain sweet mouths which must bear the mean or middle part: and so with these three parts of music you shall make your cry perfect: and herein you shall observe that these hounds thus mixed do run just and even together, and not hang off loose one from another, which is the vilest sight

II. *An Elizabethan Huntsman*

that may be, and you shall understand that this composition is best to be made of the swiftest and largest deep-mouthed dog, the slowest middle sized dog, and the shortest-legged slender dog; and if amongst these you cast in a couple or two of small singing beagles, which as small trebles may warble amongst them, the cry will be a great deal the sweeter....

If you would have your kennel for depth of mouth, then you shall compound it of the largest dogs, which have the greatest mouths and deepest flews, such as your west-country Cheshire and Lancashire dogs are, and to five or six couple of bass mouths you shall not add above two couple of counter-tenors, as many means, and not above one couple of roarers, which being heard but now and then, as at the opening or hitting of a scent, will give much sweetness to the solemnness and graveness of the cry, and the music thereof will be much more delightful to the ears of every beholder.

GERVASE MARKHAM, *Countrey Contentments*, 1611

Football (a puritan view)

Am I so round with you as you with me,
That like a football you do spurn me thus?
You spurn me hence, and he will spurn me hither:
If I last in this service, you must case me in leather.

The Comedy of Errors, II. i. 82–85

For as concerning football playing, I protest unto you it may rather be called a friendly kind of fight, than a play or recreation; a bloody and murdering practice, than a fellowly sport or pastime. For doth not every one lie in wait for his adversary, seeking to overthrow him and to pick him on his nose, though it be upon hard stones, in ditch or dale, in valley or hill, or what place soever it be he careth not, so he have him down. And he that can serve the most of this fashion, he is counted the only fellow, and who but he? So that by this means, sometimes their necks are broken, sometimes their backs, sometimes their legs, sometime their arms, sometime one part thrust out of joint, sometime another, sometime their noses gush out with blood, sometime their eyes start out, and sometimes hurt in one place, sometimes in another. But whosoever scapeth away the best goeth not scot-free, but is either sore wounded, and bruised, so as he dieth of it, or else scapeth very hardly. And no marvel, for they have sleights to meet one betwixt two, to dash him against the heart with their elbows, to hit him under the short ribs with their gripped fists, and with their knees to catch him upon the hip, and to pick him on his neck, with an hundred such murdering devices. And hereof groweth envy, malice, rancour, choler, hatred, displeasure, enmity and what not else: and sometimes fighting, brawling, contention, quarrel picking, murder, homicide and great effusion of blood, as experience daily teacheth.

Philip Stubbes, *The Anatomie of Abuses*, 1583 (2nd ed.)

A local play

The interest of this piece lies in the fact that the author was born in the same year as Shakespeare, 1564. Similar plays were no doubt given at Stratford. The play described is a "Morality".

In the city of Gloucester, the manner is (as I think it is in other like corporations) that when players of interludes come to town, they first attend the mayor, to inform him what nobleman's servants they are, and so to get licence for their public playing; and if the mayor like the actors, or would shew respect to their lord and master, he appoints them to play their first play before himself and the aldermen and common council of the city; and that is called the mayor's play, where everyone that will comes in without money, the mayor giving the players a reward as he thinks fit to shew respect unto them. At such a play my father took me with him, and made me stand between his legs, as he sat upon one of the benches, where we saw and heard very well. The play was called *The Cradle of Security*, wherein was personated a king or some great prince, with his courtiers of several kinds, amongst which three ladies were in special grace with him; and they keeping him in delights and pleasures, drew him from his graver counsellors, hearing of sermons, and listening to good counsel and admonitions, that in the end they got him to lie down in a cradle upon the stage, where these three ladies joining in a sweet song rocked him asleep, that he snorted again, and in the meantime closely conveyed under the cloths wherewithal he was covered, a vizard like a swine's snout upon his face, with three wire chains fastened thereunto, the other end whereof being holden severally by those three ladies, who fall to singing again, and then discovered his face, that the spectators might see how they had transformed him, going on with their singing. Whilst all this was acting, there came forth of another door at the farthest end of the stage, two old men, the one in blue, with a sergeant at arms, his mace on his shoulder, the other in red, with a drawn sword in his hand, and leaning with the other hand upon the other's shoulder; and so they two went along in a soft pace round about by the skirt of the stage, till at last they came to the cradle, when all the court was in greatest jollity; and then the foremost old man with his mace stroke a fearful blow upon the cradle; whereat all the courtiers, with the three ladies and the vizard, all vanished; and the desolate prince starting up barefaced, and finding himself thus sent for to judgment, made a lamentable complaint of his miserable case, and so was carried away by wicked spirits. This prince did personate in the moral, the wicked of the world; the three ladies, Pride, Covetousness, and Luxury; the two old men, the end of the world, and the last judgment.

This sight took such impression in me, that when I came towards man's estate it was as fresh in my memory, as if I had seen it newly acted. From whence I observe out of mine own experience, what great care should be had in the education of children, to keep them from seeing of spectacles of ill examples, and hearing of lascivious or scurrilous words; for that their young memories are like fair writing-tables, wherein if the fair sentences or lessons of grace be written, they may (by God's blessing) keep them from many vicious blots of life, wherewithal they may otherwise be tainted....And withal we may observe, how far unlike the plays and harmless morals of former times are to those which have succeeded; many of which (by report of others) may be termed schoolmasters of vice, and provocations to corruptions.

R. Willis, *Mount Tabor*, 1639

§ 3. FESTIVAL

Christmas Day

Some say that ever 'gainst that season comes
Wherein our Saviour's birth is celebrated,
The bird of dawning singeth all night long:
And then, they say, no spirit can walk abroad;
The nights are wholesome; then no planets strike,
No fairy takes, nor witch hath power to charm,
So hallow'd and so gracious is the time.

Hamlet, I. i. 158–164

It is now Christmas, and not a cup of drink must pass without a carol; the beasts, fowl, and fish, come to a general execution; and the corn is ground to dust for the bakehouse, and the pastry. Cards and dice purge many a purse, and the youth shew their agility in shoeing of the wild mare. Now "Good cheer" and "Welcome", and "God be with you", and "I thank you", and "Against the new year", provide for the presents. The Lord of Misrule is no mean man for his time, and the guests of the high table must lack no wine. The lusty bloods must look about them like men, and piping and dancing puts away much melancholy. Stolen venison is sweet, and a fat coney is worth money. Pit-falls are now set for small birds, and a woodcock hangs himself in a gin. A good fire heats all the house, and a full alms-basket makes the beggars prayers. The masquers and mummers make the merry sport: but if they lose their money, their drum goes dead. Swearers and swaggerers are sent away to the ale-house, and unruly wenches go in danger of judgment. Musicians now make their instruments speak out, and a good song is worth the hearing. In sum, it is a holy time, a duty in Christians for the remembrance of Christ, and custom among friends for the maintenance of good fellowship.

NICHOLAS BRETON, *Fantastickes,* 1626

May-day (a puritan view)

They rose up early to observe
The rite of May.

A Midsummer Night's Dream, IV. i. 138–139

Against May, Whitsunday, or some other time of the year, every parish, town and village assemble themselves together, both men, women and children, old and young, even all indifferently; and either going all together or dividing themselves into companies, they go some to the woods and groves, some to the hills and mountains, some to one place and some to another, where they spend all the night in pleasant pastimes; and in the morning they return, bringing with them birch boughs and branches of trees, to deck their assemblies withal. And no marvel, for there is a great lord present amongst them, as superintendent and lord over their pastimes and sports, namely Sathan, prince of hell. But their chiefest jewel they bring from thence is their May-pole, which they bring home with great veneration, as thus. They have twenty or forty yoke of oxen, every ox having a sweet nose-gay of flowers placed on the tip of his horns; and these oxen draw home this May-pole (this stinking idol, rather) which is covered all over with flowers and herbs, bound round about with strings from the top to the bottom, and sometime painted with variable colours, with two or three hundred men, women and children following it with great devotion. And thus being reared up with handkerchiefs and flags streaming on the top, they straw the ground about, bind green boughs about it, set up summer-halls, bowers, and arbours hard by it; and then they fall to banquet and feast, to leap and dance about it, as the heathen people did at the dedication of their idols, whereof this is a perfect pattern, or rather the thing itself.

PHILIP STUBBES, *The Anatomie of Abuses*, 1583 (2nd ed.)

The country in winter

I

When icicles hang by the wall,
  And Dick the shepherd blows his nail,
And Tom bears logs into the hall,
  And milk comes frozen home in pail,
When blood is nipp'd, and ways be foul,
Then nightly sings the staring owl,
                    Tu-who;
  Tu-whit, tu-who—a merry note,
  While greasy Joan doth keel the pot.

II

When all aloud the wind doth blow,
  And coughing drowns the parson's saw,
And birds sit brooding in the snow,
  And Marian's nose looks red and raw,
When roasted crabs hiss in the bowl,
Then nightly sings the staring owl,
                    Tu-who;
  Tu-whit, tu-who—a merry note,
  While greasy Joan doth keel the pot.

Love's Labour's Lost, v. ii. 902–937

§ 4. SUPERSTITION

Witchcraft

                    What are these,
So wither'd and so wild in their attire,
That look not like th' inhabitants o' the earth,
And yet are on't? Live you? or are you aught
That man may question? You seem to understand me,
By each at once her choppy finger laying
Upon her skinny lips: you should be women,
And yet your beards forbid me to interpret
That you are so.

Macbeth, I. iii. 39–47

The witches' cauldron

Double, double toil and trouble;
Fire burn and cauldron bubble.

Macbeth, IV. i. 10–11

Then he (the Devil) teacheth them to make ointments of the flesh of children, whereby they ride in the air, and accomplish all their desires. So as, if there be any children unbaptised, or not guarded with the sign of the cross, or orisons; then the witches may and do catch them from their mothers' sides in the night, or out of their cradles, or otherwise kill them with their ceremonies; and after burial steal them out of their graves, and seethe them in a cauldron, until their flesh be made potable. Of the thickest whereof they make ointments, whereby they ride in the air; but the thinner potion they put into flagons, whereof whosoever drinketh, observing certain ceremonies, immediately becometh a master or rather a mistress in that practice and faculty.

REGINALD SCOT, *The Discoverie of Witchcraft*, 1584

Transformation

Snout. O Bottom, thou art changed! what do I see on thee?
Bottom. What do you see? you see an ass-head of your own, do you?
Quince. Bless thee, Bottom! bless thee! thou art translated.

A Midsummer Night's Dream, III. i. 120–125

It happened in the city of Salamin, in the kingdom of Cyprus (wherein is a good haven), that a ship loaden with merchandize stayed there for a short space. In the mean time many of the soldiers and mariners went to shore, to provide fresh victuals. Among which number, a certain Englishman, being a sturdy young fellow, went to a woman's house, a little way out of the city, and not far from the sea side, to see whether she had any eggs to sell. Who perceiving him to be a lusty young fellow, a stranger, and far from his country (so as upon the loss of him there would be the less miss or inquiry), she considered with herself how to destroy him; and willed him to stay there awhile, whilst she went to fetch a few eggs for him. But she tarried long, so as the young man called unto her, desiring her to make haste: for he told her that the tide would be spent, and by that means his ship would be gone, and leave him behind. Howbeit, after some detracting of time, she brought him a few eggs, willing him to return to her, if his ship were gone when he came. The young fellow returned towards his ship: but before he went aboard, he would needs eat an egg or twain to satisfy his hunger, and within short space he became dumb and out of his wits (as he afterwards said). When he would have entered into the ship, the mariners beat him back with a cudgel, saying: "What a murrain lacks the ass? Whither the devil will this ass?" The ass or young man (I cannot tell by which name I should term him) being many times repelled, and understanding their words that called him ass, considering that he could speak never a word, and yet could understand every body, he thought that he was bewitched by the woman, at whose house he was. And therefore, when by no means he could get into the boat, but was driven to tarry and see her departure, being also beaten from place to place as an ass, he remembered the witch's words, and the words of his own fellows that called him ass, and returned to the witch's house, in whose service he remained by the space of three years, doing nothing with his hands all that while, but carried such burdens as she laid on his back; having only this comfort, that although he were reputed an ass among strangers and beasts, yet that both this witch, and all other witches knew him to be a man.

REGINALD SCOT, *The Discoverie of Witchcraft*, 1584

Fairyland

But we are spirits of another sort.

A Midsummer Night's Dream, III. ii. 388

Either I mistake your shape and making quite
Or else you are that shrewd and knavish sprite
Call'd Robin Goodfellow: are not you he
That frights the maidens of the villagery;
Skim milk, and sometimes labour in the quern
And bootless make the breathless housewife churn;
And sometime make the drink to bear no barm;
Mislead night-wanderers, laughing at their harm?
Those that Hobgoblin call you and sweet Puck,
You do their work, and they shall have good luck:
Are not you he? *Ibid.* II. i. 32–42

The little book from which the following extracts are taken has been described as the most valuable and important contemporary illustration of *A Midsummer Night's Dream.*

How King Oberon called Robin Good-fellow to dance

King Oberon, seeing Robin Good-fellow do so many honest and merry tricks, called him one night out of his bed with these words, saying:

Robin, my son, come quickly rise:
First stretch, then yawn, and rub your eyes;
For thou must go with me to-night,
To see, and taste of my delight.
Quickly come, my wanton son;
'Twere time our sports were now begun.

Robin, hearing this, rose and went to him. There were with King Oberon a many fairies, all attired in green silk: all these, with King Oberon, did welcome Robin Good-fellow into their company. Oberon took Robin by the hand and led him a dance. Their musician was little Tom Thumb, for he had an excellent bag-pipe made of a wren's quill and the skin of a Greenland louse. This pipe was so shrill, and so sweet, that a Scottish pipe, compared to it, it would no more come near it, than a Jew's-trump doth to an Irish harp. After they had danced, King Oberon spake to his son, Robin Good-fellow, in this manner:

Whene'er thou hear my piper blow,
From thy bed see that thou go;
For nightly you must with us dance,
When we in circles round do prance.
I love thee, son, and by the hand
I carry thee to Fairy Land,
Where thou shalt see what no man knows:
Such love to thee King Oberon owes.

So marched they in good manner, with their piper before, to the Fairy Land: there did King Oberon shew Robin Good-fellow many secrets, which he never did open to the world.

The tricks of the fairy called Pinch

After that we have danced in this manner as you have beheld, I, that am called Pinch, do go about from house to house. Sometimes I find the doors of the house open. That negligent servant that left them so, I do so nip him or her, that with my pinches their bodies are as many colours as a mackerel's back....

Sometimes I find a slut sleeping in the chimney corner, when she should be washing of her dishes, or doing something else which she hath left undone: her I pinch about the arms, for not laying her arms to her labour. Some I find in their bed snorting and sleeping, and their houses lying as clean as a nasty dog's kennel; in one corner bones, in another egg-shells, behind the door a heap of dust, the dishes under feet, and the cat in the cupboard: all these sluttish tricks I do reward with blue legs, and blue arms. I find some slovens too, as well as sluts: they pay for their beastliness too, as well as the women-kind; for if they uncase a sloven and not untie their points, I so pay their arms that they cannot sometimes untie them, if they would. Those that leave foul shoes, or go into their beds with their stockings on, I use them as I did the former, and never leave them till they have left their beastliness.

But to the good I do no harm,
But cover them, and keep them warm:
Sluts and slovens I do pinch,
And make them in their beds to wince.
This is my practice, and my trade.
Many have I cleanly made.

The tricks of the fairy called Gull

When mortals keep their beds I walk abroad, and for my pranks am called by the name of Gull. I with a feigned voice do often deceive many men, to their great amazement. Many times I get on men and women, and so lie on their stomachs, that I cause them great pain, for which they call me by the name of Hag, or Night-mare. 'Tis I that do steal children, and in the place of them leave changelings. Sometimes I also steal milk and cream, and then with my brothers Patch, Pinch, and Grim, and sisters Sib, Tib, Lick, and Lull, I feast with my stolen goods. Our little piper hath his share in all our spoils, but neither he nor our women fairies do ever put themselves in danger to do any great exploit.

What Gull can do, I have you shown;
I am inferior unto none.
Command me, Robin, thou shalt know,
That I for thee will ride or go:
I can do greater things than these
Upon the land, and on the seas.

The tricks of the fairy called Grim

I walk with the owl, and make many to cry as loud as she doth holloa. Sometimes I do affright many simple people, for which some have termed me the Black Dog of Newgate. At the meeting of young men and maids I many times am, and when they are in the midst of all their good cheer, I come in, in some fearful shape, and affright them, and then carry away their good cheer, and eat it with my fellow fairies. 'Tis I that do, like a screech-owl, cry at sick men's windows, which makes the hearers so fearful, that they say that the sick person cannot live. Many other ways have I to fright the simple, but the understanding man I cannot move to fear, because he knows I have no power to do hurt.

Robin Good-fellow; his mad prankes and merry jests, 1628

I'll follow you, I'll lead you about a round,
Through bog, through bush, through brake, through brier:
Sometime a horse I'll be, sometime a hound,
A hog, a headless bear, sometime a fire;
And neigh, and bark, and grunt, and roar, and burn,
Like horse, hound, hog, bear, fire, at every turn.

A Midsummer Night's Dream, III. i. 112–117

Where the bee sucks, there suck I:
In a cowslip's bell I lie;
There I couch when owls do cry.
On the bat's back I do fly
After summer merrily:
Merrily, merrily shall I live now
Under the blossom that hangs on the bough.

The Tempest, v. i. 88–94

§ 5. SCHOOL

At first the infant,
Mewling and puking in the nurse's arms.
And then the whining schoolboy, with his satchel
And shining morning face, creeping like snail
Unwillingly to school. *As You Like It*, II. vii. 143–147

The school day

Philoponus. The school-time should begin at six....

Spoudeus. Would you then have the master and usher present so early?

Philoponus. The usher should necessarily be there to be present amongst them, though he follow his own private study that hour, yet to see that all the scholars do their duties appointed, and that there be no disorder: which will be, unless he or some other of authority be amongst them. For otherwise the best children, left to their own liberty, will shew themselves children. If the master be present at seven it may suffice, where there is any in his place, whose presence they stand in awe of.

Spoudeus. But it is hard for the little children to rise so early, and in some families all lie long: how would you have them come so soon then? You would not have them beaten every time they come over-late, as the custom is in some schools.

Philoponus. That I take far too great severity and whereby many a poor child is driven into wonderful fear, and either to play the truant, or make some device to leave the school; at least to come with a marvellous ill will, and oft to be dragged to school, to the reproach of the master and the school. The best means that ever I could find to make them to rise early, to prevent all this fear of whipping, is this: by letting the little ones to have their places in their forms daily, according to their coming after six of the clock. So many as are there at six, to have their places as they had them by election on the day before. All who come after six, every one to sit as he cometh, and so to continue that day and until he recover his place again by the election of the form or otherwise. Thus deal with them at all times, after every intermission, when they are to be in their places again and you shall have them ever attending who to be first in his place. So greatly even children are provoked by the credit of their places. If any cannot be brought by this, then to be noted in the black bill by a special mark, and feel the punishment thereof: and sometimes present correction to be used for terror; though this (as I said) to be more seldom, for making them to fear coming to the school.

The higher scholars must of necessity rest to do their exercises, if their exercises be strictly called for. Thus they are to continue until nine, signified by monitors, subdoctor, or otherwise. Then at nine I find that order which is in Westminster to be far the best; to let them to have a quarter of an hour at least, or more for intermission, either for breakfast, for all who are near unto the school, that can be there within the time limited, or else for the necessity of everyone, or their honest recreation, or to prepare their exercises against the master's coming in.

After, each of them to be in his place in an instant upon the knocking of the door or some other sign given by the subdoctor or monitors, in pain of loss of his place, or further punishment, as was noted before; so to continue until eleven of the clock; or somewhat after, to countervail the time of the intermission at nine.

To be again all ready and in their places at one, in an instant; to continue until three or half an hour after: then to have another quarter of an hour or more, as at nine, for drinking and necessities. So to continue till half an hour after five, thereby in that half hour to countervail the time at three. Then to end so as was showed, with reading a piece of a chapter and with singing two staves of a psalm: lastly with prayer to be used by the master....

Spoudeus. But these intermissions at nine and three may be offensive. They who know not the manner of them may reproach the school, thinking that they do nothing but play.

Philoponus. We are, so much as may be, in all things to avoid offence. But when by long custom the order is once made known, it will be no more offensive than it is at Westminster, or than it is at noon and night; so that it be done in a decent order....

Besides those and all other their intermissions, it is very requisite also that they should have weekly one part of an afternoon for recreation, as a reward of their diligence, obedience and profiting: and that to be appointed at the master's discretion, either the Thursday after the usual custom, or according to the best opportunity of the place. That also to be procured by some verses made by the victors, as was shewed: and then only when there hath been already no play-day in the week before nor holy day in all the week. . . .

All recreations and sports of scholars would be meet for gentlemen. Clownish sports, or perilous, or yet playing for money are no way to be admitted. The recreations of the studious are as well to be looked unto, as the study of the rest: that none take hurt by his study, either for mind or body, or any way else.

Yet here of the other side, very great care is to be had in the moderating of their recreation. For schools, generally, do not take more hindrance by any one thing, than by over-often leave to play. Experience teacheth that this draweth their minds utterly away from their books, that they cannot take pains, for longing after play and talking of it; as also devising means to procure others to get leave to play: so that ordinarily when they are but in hope thereof, they will do things very negligently; and after the most play they are evermore far the worst.

JOHN BRINSLEY, *Ludus Literarius or the Grammar Schoole*, 1612

Punishment

First to begin with the lesser kinds of punishments; and so by degrees to the highest and severest, after this manner observing carefully the natures of everyone, as was said:

1. To use reproofs; and those sometimes more sharp according to the nature of the offender and his fault.

2. To punish by loss of place to him who doth better according to our discretion.

3. To punish by a note, which may be called the black bill. This I would have the principal punishment, I mean most of use. For you shall find by experience, that it being rightly used, it is more available than all other, to keep all in obedience; and specially for any notoriously idle or stubborn, or which are of evil behaviour any way....

4. Sometimes in greater faults, to give three or four jerks with a birch, or with a small red willow where birch cannot be had. Or for terror in some notorious fault, half a dozen stripes or more, soundly laid on, according to the discretion of the master. Some do only keep a bill, and note carefully their several principal disorders; and now and then, shew them their names and faults mildly, how oft they have been admonished, and when they take them in hand pay them soundly and by this policy keep them in great obedience.

In this correction with the rod, special provision must be had for sundry things.

I. That when you are to correct any stubborn or unbroken boy, you may be sure with him to hold him fast; as they are enforced to do, who are to shoe or to tame an unbroken colt. To this end appoint three or four of your scholars, whom you know to be honest, and strong enough, or more if need be, to lay hands upon him together, to hold him fast, over some form, so that he cannot stir hand nor foot; or else if no other remedy will serve, to hold him to some post (which is far the safest and free from inconvenience) so as he cannot anyway hurt himself or others, be he never so peevish. Neither that he can have hope by any device or turning, or by his apparel, or any other means to escape. Nor yet that any one be left in his stubbornness to go away murmuring, pouting, or blowing and puffing, until he shew as much submission as any, and that he will lie still of himself without any holding; yet so as ever a wise moderation be kept....

II. To be wary for smiting them over the backs, in any case, or in such sort as in any way to hurt or endanger them....

III. That the master do not in any case abase himself to strive or struggle with any boy to take him up: but to appoint other of the strongest to do it, where such need is, in such sort as was shewed before; and the rather for fear of hurting them in his anger, and for the evils which may come thereof and which some schoolmasters have lamented after.

IV. That the masters and ushers also do by all means avoid all furious anger, threatening, chasing, fretting, reviling: for these things will diminish authority and may do much hurt, and much endanger many ways. And therefore on the contrary, that all their correction be done with authority, and with a wise and sober moderation, in a demonstration of duty to God and love to the children, for their amendment, and the reformation of their evil manners.

JOHN BRINSLEY, *Ludus Literarius or the Grammar Schoole*, 1612

III

LONDON

We do not know when Shakespeare left Stratford for London. But as his youngest children, a twin boy and girl, were born at Stratford in 1585 and he had already become a famous London playwright by 1592, it was probably at some time between those dates. Legend says that he went up to seek his fortune because his father had somehow lost much of his money. If so, he probably walked all the way. Walking, indeed, was the usual means of getting from place to place in those days. People who could afford it went on horseback; ladies and elderly people drove in coaches or horse-litters; and great men and officials in a hurry "rode post". The passages that follow will give an idea of the life of the roads and the noise, disorder and splendour of Elizabethan London.

§ 1. THE ROAD TO LONDON

Jog on, jog on the foot-path way,
And merrily hent the stile-a:
A merry heart goes all the day,
Your sad tires in a mile-a.

The Winter's Tale, IV. ii. 133–136

The highways of England

Now to speak generally of our common highways through the English part of the isle (for of the rest I can say nothing), you shall understand that in the clay or cledgy soil they are often very deep and troublesome in the winter half. Wherefore by authority of parliament an order is taken for their yearly amendment, whereby all sorts of the common people do employ their travail for six days in summer upon the same. And albeit that the intent of the statute is very profitable for the reparations of the decayed places, yet the rich do so cancel their portions, and the poor so loiter in their labours, that of all the six, scarcely two good days' work are well performed and accomplished in a parish on these so necessary affairs. Besides this, such as have land lying upon the sides of the ways do utterly neglect to ditch and scour their drains and water-courses for better avoidance of the winter waters (except it may be set off or cut from the meaning of the statute), whereby the streets do grow to be much more gulled than before, and thereby very noisome for such as travel by the same.... Finally, this is another thing likewise to be considered of, that the trees and bushes growing by the streets' sides do not a little keep off the force of the sun in summer for drying up of the lanes. Wherefore if order were taken that their boughs should continually be kept short, and the bushes not suffered to spread so far into the narrow paths, that inconvenience would also be remedied, and many a slough prove hard ground that yet is deep and hollow.

William Harrison, *Description of England*, 1587 (2nd ed.)

The Cambridge to London road

On the road we passed through a villainous boggy and wild country and several times missed our way

III. *The Southwark Gate of London Bridge*

because the country thereabouts is very little inhabited and is nearly a waste; and there is one spot in particular where the mud is so deep that in my opinion it would scarcely be possible to pass with a coach in winter or in rainy weather.

Visit of Frederick, Duke of Würtemberg, 1592 [Rye]

Carriers early astir

SCENE. *Rochester. An Inn-yard*

Gadshill. Good morrow, carriers. What's o'clock?

First Carrier. I think it be two o'clock.

Gadshill. I prithee, lend me thy lanthorn, to see my gelding in the stable.

Second Carrier. ...Lend me thy lanthorn, quoth a'? marry, I'll see thee hanged first.

Gadshill. Sirrah carrier, what time do you mean to come to London?

Second Carrier. Time enough to go to bed with a candle, I warrant thee. Come, neighbour Mugs, we'll call up the gentlemen: they will along with company, for they have great charge.

1 *Henry IV*, II. i. 36–51

The Post

In England towards the south, and in the west parts, and from London to Berwick upon the confines of Scotland, post-horses are established at every ten miles or thereabouts, which they ride a false gallop after some ten miles an hour sometimes, and that makes their hire the greater: for with a commission from the chief post-master, or chief lords of the Council (given either upon public business, or at least pretence thereof) a passenger shall pay two-pence halfpenny each mile for his horse, and as much for his guide's horse: but one guide will serve the whole company, though many ride together, who may easily bring back the horses, driving them before him, who know the way as well as a beggar knows his dish. They which have no such commission pay threepence for each mile. This extraordinary charge of horses' hire may well be recompensed with the speed of the journey, whereby greater expenses in the inns are avoided. All the difficulty is to have a body able to endure the toil. For these horses the passenger is at no charge to give them meat, only at the ten miles' end the boy that carries them back will expect some few pence in gift.

FYNES MORYSON, *Itinerary*, 1617

Inns

Servants in league with highwaymen

Chamberlain. Good morrow, Master Gadshill. It holds current that I told you yesternight: there's a franklin in the wild of Kent hath brought three hundred marks with him in gold: I heard him tell it to one of his company last night at supper; a kind of auditor; one that hath abundance of charge too, God knows what. They are up already and call for eggs and butter: they will away presently.

* * * * * *

Gadshill. Give me thy hand: thou shalt have a share in our purchase, as I am a true man.

Chamberlain. Nay, rather let me have it, as you are a false thief.

1 *Henry IV*, II. i. 58–103

Those towns that we call thoroughfares have great and sumptuous inns builded in them for the receiving of such travellers and strangers as pass to and fro. The manner of harbouring wherein is not like to that of some other countries in which the host or goodman of the house doth challenge a lordly authority over his guests, but clean otherwise, sith every man may use his inn as his own house in England and have for his money how great or little variety of victuals, and what other service himself shall think expedient to call for. Our inns are also very well furnished with napery, bedding and tapestry, especially with napery: for beside the linen used at the tables, which is commonly washed daily, is such and so much as belongeth unto the estate and calling of the guest. Each comer is sure to lie in clean sheets, wherein no man hath been lodged since they came from the laundress or out of the water wherein they were last washed. If the traveller have an horse, his bed doth cost him nothing, but if he go on foot he is sure to pay a penny for the same: but whether he be horseman or footman if his chamber be once appointed he may carry the key with him, as of his own house, so long as he lodgeth there. If he lose ought whilst he abideth in the inn, the host is bound by a general custom to restore the damage, so that there is no greater security anywhere for travellers than in the greatest inns of England. Their horses in like sort are walked, dressed and looked unto by certain hostlers or hired servants, appointed at the charges of the goodman of the house, who in hope of extraordinary reward will deal very diligently, after outward appearance, in this their function and calling. Herein nevertheless are many of them blameworthy, in that they do not only deceive the beast oftentimes of his allowance by sundry means, except their owners look well to them; but also make such packs with slipper merchants which hunt after prey (for what place is sure from evil and wicked persons?) that many an honest man is spoiled of his goods as he travelleth to and fro, in which feat also the counsel of the tapsters or drawers of drink and chamberlains is not seldom behind or wanting. Certes I believe that not a chapman or traveller in England is robbed by the way without the knowledge of some of them; for when he cometh into the inn, and alighteth from his horse, the hostler forthwith is very busy to take down his budget or capcase in the yard from his saddle-bow, which he peiseth slyly in his hand to feel the weight thereof: or if he miss of this pitch, when the guest hath taken up his chamber, the chamberlain that looketh to the making of the beds will be sure to remove it from the place where the owner hath set it, as if it were to set it more conveniently somewhere else, whereby he getteth an inkling whether it be money or other sort wares, and thereof giveth warning to such odd guests as haunt the house and are of his confederacy, to the utter undoing of many an honest yeoman as he journeyeth by the way....

In all our inns we have plenty of ale, beer and sundry kinds of wine, and such is the capacity of some of them that they are able to lodge two hundred or three hundred persons and their horses at ease, and thereto with a very short warning make such provision for their diet, as to him that is unacquainted withal may seem to be incredible. Howbeit of all in England there are no worse inns than in London, and yet many are there far better than the best that I have heard of in any foreign country, if all circumstances be duly considered....And it is a world to see how each owner of them contendeth with other for goodness of entertainment of their guests, as about fineness and change of linen, furniture of bedding, beauty of rooms, service at the table, costliness of plate, strength of drink, variety of wines, or well using of horses. Finally there is not so much omitted among them as the gorgeousness of their very signs at their doors, wherein some do consume thirty or forty pounds, a mere vanity in mine opinion; but so vain will they needs be, and that not only to give some outward token of the inn-keeper's wealth, but also to procure good guests to the frequenting of their houses in hope there to be well used.

William Harrison, *Description of England*, 1587 (2nd ed.)

Highwaymen on Gadshill

First Traveller. Come, neighbour; the boy shall lead our horses down the hill; we'll walk afoot awhile, and ease our legs.

Thieves. Stand!

Travellers. Jesu bless us!

Falstaff. Strike; down with them; cut the villains' throats: ah! whoreson caterpillars! bacon-fed knaves! they hate us youth: down with them; fleece them. 1 *Henry IV*, II. ii. 86–95

Afterwards his Highness rode back again [from Rochester] to Gravesend, the night being as dark as pitch and the wind high and boisterous; he slept there that night. On the road, however, an Englishman, with a drawn sword in his hand, came upon us unawares and ran after us as fast as he could; perhaps he expected to find other persons, for it is very probable that he had an ambush, as that particular part of the road is not the most safe.

Visit of Frederick, Duke of Würtemberg, 1592 [Rye]

§ 2. ROGUES AND VAGABONDS ON THE ROAD

There are cozeners abroad; therefore it behoves men to be wary. *The Winter's Tale*, IV. iii. 256

To have an open ear, a quick eye, and a nimble hand, is necessary for a cut-purse: a good nose is requisite also, to smell out work for the other senses. I see this is the time that the unjust man doth thrive....Every lane's end, every shop, church, session, hanging, yields a careful man work.

Ibid. IV. iii. 686–704

Fraternities of vagabonds

A gentleman of late hath taken great pains to search out the secret practices of this ungracious rabble. And among other things he setteth down and describeth three and twenty sorts of them whose names it shall not be amiss to remember whereby each one may take occasion to read and know as also by his industry what wicked people they are, and what villainy remaineth in them.

The several disorders and degrees amongst our idle vagabonds.*

1. Rufflers.
2. Uprightmen.
3. Hookers or anglers.
4. Rogues.
5. Wild rogues.
6. Priggers of prancers.
7. Palliards.
8. Fraters.
9. Abrams.
10. Freshwater mariners or whipjacks.
11. Dummerers.
12. Drunken tinkers.
13. Swaddlers or pedlars.
14. Jarkmen or patricoes.

Of the women kind.

1. Demanders for glimmer or fire.
2. Bawdy-baskets.
3. Morts.
4. Autem morts.
5. Walking morts.
6. Doxies.
7. Dells.
8. Kinching morts.
9. Kinching coes.

WILLIAM HARRISON, *Description of England*, 1587 (2nd ed.)

(i) *Abraham men*

Edgar. My face I'll grime with filth,
Blanket my loins, elf all my hair in knots,
And with presented nakedness out-face
The winds and persecutions of the sky.
The country gives me proof and precedent
Of Bedlam beggars, who, with roaring voices,
Strike in their numb'd and mortified bare arms
Pins, wooden pricks, nails, sprigs of rosemary;

* See glossary under "Rogues".

And with this horrible object, from low farms,
Poor pelting villages, sheep-cotes, and mills,
Sometime with lunatic bans, sometime with prayers,
Enforce their charity. Poor Turlygood! poor Tom!

King Lear, II. iii. 9–20

These Abraham men be those that feign themselves to have been mad and have been kept either in Bethlehem or in some other prison a good time, and not amongst twenty that ever came in prison for any such cause: yet will they say how piteously and most extremely they have been beaten and dealt withal. Some of these be merry and very pleasant, they will dance and sing; some others be as cold and reasonable to talk withal. These beg money, either when they come at farmer's houses they will demand bacon, either cheese or wool or anything that is worth money. And if they espy small company within, they will with fierce countenance demand somewhat, where for fear the maids will give them largely to be rid of them....

(ii) *Rufflers on Shooter's Hill*

The story below, it has been observed, is quite in the manner of Falstaff's escapades.

I had of late years an old man to my tenant, who customably a great time went twice in the week to London, either with fruit or with peascods, when time served therefore. And as he was coming homewards on Blackheath, at the end thereof next to Shooter's Hill, he overtook two rufflers, the one mannerly waiting on the other, as one had been the master, and the other the man or servant carrying his master's cloak. This old man was very glad that he might have their company over the hill, because that day he had made a good market; for he had seven shillings in his purse, and an old angel, which this poor man had thought had not been in his purse, for he willed his wife over night to take out the same angel and lay it up until his coming home again. And he verily thought that his wife had so done, which indeed forgot to do it. Thus after salutations had, this master ruffler entered into communication with this simple old man, who, riding softly beside them, communed of many matters. Thus feeding this old man with pleasant talk, until they were on the top of the hill, where these rufflers might well behold the coast about them clear, quickly steps unto this poor man, and taketh hold of his horse bridle, and leadeth him into the wood, and demandeth of him what and how much money he had in his purse. "Now, by my troth", quoth this old man; "you are a merry gentleman. I know you mean not to take away anything from me, but rather to give me some if I should ask it of you." By and by, this servant thief casteth the cloak that he carried on his arm about this poor man's face, that he should not mark or view them, with sharp words to deliver quickly that he had, and to confess truly what was in his purse. This poor man, then all abashed, yielded and confessed that he had but just seven shillings in his purse; and the truth is he knew of no more. This old angel was fallen out of a little purse into the bottom of a great purse. Now, this seven shillings in white money they quickly found, thinking indeed that there had been no more; yet farther groping and searching found this old angel. And with great admiration, this gentleman thief began to bless him, saying, "Good Lord, what a world is this! how may," quoth he, "a man believe or trust in the same? See you not," quoth he, "this old knave told me that he had but seven shillings, and here is more by an angel: what an old knave and a false knave have we here!" quoth this ruffler, "Our Lord have mercy on us, will this world never be better?"—and therewith went their way, and left the old man in the wood, doing him no more harm. But sorrowfully sighing, this old man, returning home, declared his misadventure, with all the words and circumstances above shewed....

(iii) *A hooker or angler*

These hookers, or anglers, be perilous and most wicked knaves, and be derived or proceed forth from the uprightmen. They commonly go in frieze jerkins and gally-slops, pointed beneath the knee. These when they practise their pilfering, it is all by night; for, as they walk a-day-times from house to house, to demand charity, they vigilantly mark where or in what place they may attain to their prey, casting their eyes up to every window, well noting what they see there, whether apparel or linen, hanging near unto the said windows, and that will they be sure to have the next night following. For they customably carry with them a staff of five or six foot long, in which, within one inch of the top thereof, is a little hole bored through, in which hole they put an iron hook, and with the same they will pluck unto them quickly anything that they may reach therewith, which hook in the daytime they covertly carry about them, and is never seen or taken out till they come to the place where they work their feat. Such have I seen at my house, and have oft talked with them and have handled their staves, not then understanding to what use or intent they served, although I had and perceived, by their talk and behaviour, great likelihood of evil suspicion in them. They will either lean upon their staff, to hide the hole thereof, when they talk with you, or hold their hand upon the hole; and what stuff, either woollen or linen, they thus hook out, they never carry the same forthwith to their stauling-kens, but hide the same a three days in some secret corner, and after convey the same to their houses abovesaid, where their host or hostess giveth them money for the same, but half the value that it is worth. . . . I was credibly informed that a hooker came to a farmer's house in the dead of the night, and putting back a draw-window of a low chamber, the bed standing hard by the said window, in which lay three persons (a man and two big boys), this hooker with his staff plucked off their garments which lay upon them to keep them warm, with the coverlet and sheet, and left them lying asleep naked saving their shirts, and had away all clean, and never could understand where it became. I verily suppose that when they were well waked with cold, they surely thought that Robin Goodfellow (according to the old saying) had been with them that night.

THOMAS HARMAN, *A Caveat or Warening for Commen Cursetors*, 1567

§ 3. LONDON SIGHTS AND SCENES

But now behold,
In the quick forge and working-house of thought,
How London doth pour out her citizens.

Henry V, v. chor. 22–24

A foreigner's opinion

London is a large, excellent and mighty city of business, and the most important in the whole kingdom; most of the inhabitants are employed in buying and selling merchandize, and trading in almost every corner of the world, since the river is most useful and convenient for this purpose, considering that ships from France, the Netherlands, Sweden, Denmark, Hamburg and other kingdoms, come almost up to the city, to which they convey goods and receive and take away others in exchange.

It is a very populous city, so that one can scarcely pass along the streets, on account of the throng.

IV. *Elizabethan Women*

(From left to right, two citizens' wives, a citizen's daughter, and a farmer's wife)

The inhabitants are magnificently apparelled, and are extremely proud and overbearing; and because the greater part, especially the tradespeople, seldom go into other countries, but always remain in their houses in the city attending to their business, they care little for foreigners, but scoff and laugh at them; and moreover one dare not oppose them, else the street-boys and apprentices collect together in immense crowds and strike to the right and left unmercifully without regard to person; and because they are the strongest, one is obliged to put up with the insult as well as the injury.

The women have much more liberty than perhaps in any other place; they also know well how to make use of it, for they go dressed out in exceedingly fine clothes, and give all their attention to their ruffs and stuffs, to such a degree indeed, that, as I am informed, many a one does not hesitate to wear velvet in the streets, which is common with them, whilst at home perhaps they have not a piece of dry bread. All the English women are accustomed to wear hats upon their heads, and gowns cut after the old German fashion—for indeed their descent is from the Saxons.

Visit of Frederick, Duke of Würtemberg, 1592 [Rye]

The buildings

Now at London the houses of the citizens (especially in the chief streets) are very narrow in the front towards the street, but are built five or six roofs high, commonly of timber and clay with plaster, and are very neat and commodious within: and the building of citizens' houses in other cities is not much unlike this. But withal understand that in London many stately palaces, built by noblemen upon the river Thames, do make a very great shew to them that pass by water; and that there be many more like palaces, also built towards land, but scattered and great part of them in back lanes and streets, which if they were joined to the first in good order, as other cities are built uniformly, they would make not only fair streets, but even a beautiful city, to which few might justly be preferred for the magnificence of the building. Besides that, the aldermen's and chief citizens' houses, howsoever they are stately for building, yet being built all inward, that the whole room towards the streets may be reserved for shops of tradesmen, make no shew outwardly, so as in truth all the magnificence of London building is hidden from the view of strangers at the first sight, till they have more particular view thereof by long abode there, and then they will prefer the buildings of this famous city to many that appear more stately at the first sight. FYNES MORYSON, *Itinerary*, 1617

London Bridge

The bridge at London is worthily to be numbered among the miracles of the world, if men respect the building and foundation laid artificially and stately over an ebbing and flowing water upon 21 piles of stone, with 20 arches, under which barks may pass, the lowest foundation being (as they say) packs of wool, most durable against the force of water, and not to be repaired but upon great fall of the waters and by artificial turning or stopping the recourse of them; or if men respect the houses built upon the bridge, as great and high as those of the firm land, so as a man cannot know that he passeth a bridge, but would judge himself to be in the street, save that the houses on both sides are combined in the top, making the passage somewhat dark, and that in some few open places the river of Thames may be seen on both sides. FYNES MORYSON, *Itinerary*, 1617

The noise and bustle of the streets

Why sweat they under burdens?
The Merchant of Venice, IV. i. 94

In every street, carts and coaches make such a thundering as if the world ran upon wheels: at every corner, men, women and children meet in such shoals, that posts are set up of purpose to strengthen the houses, lest with jostling one another they should shoulder them down. Besides, hammers are beating in one place, tubs hooping in another, pots clinking in a third, water-tankards running at tilt in a fourth. Here are porters sweating under burdens, their merchant's men bearing bags of money. Chapmen (as if they were at leap frog) skip out of one shop into another. Tradesmen (as if they were dancing galliards) are lusty at legs and never stand still. All are as busy as country attorneys at an assizes.

THOMAS DEKKER, *The Seuen Deadly Sinnes of London*, 1606

Constables and watchmen

Dogberry. This is your charge: you shall comprehend all vagrom men; you are to bid any man stand, in the prince's name.

Watchman. How, if a' will not stand?

Dogberry. Why, then take no note of him, but let him go; and presently call the rest of the watch together, and thank God you are rid of a knave.

Verges. If he will not stand when he is bidden, he is none of the prince's subjects.

Dogberry. True, and they are to meddle with none but the prince's subjects. You shall also make no noise in the streets: for, for the watch to babble and to talk is most tolerable and not to be endured.

Second Watchman. We will rather sleep than talk: we know what belongs to a watch.

Dogberry. Why, you speak like an ancient and most quiet watchman, for I cannot see how sleeping should offend; only, have a care that your bills be not stolen.

Much Ado About Nothing, III. iii. 25–45

A bookseller at his stall in Paul's Churchyard

If I were to paint Sloth...I swear, I would draw it like a stationer that I know, with his thumb under his girdle, who if a man come to his stall and ask him for a book, never stirs his head, or looks upon him, but stands stone still, and speaks not a word: only with his little finger points backwards to his boy, who must be his interpreter, and so all the day, gaping like a dumb image, he sits without motion, except at such times as he goes to dinner or supper: for then he is as quick as other three, eating six times every day. THOMAS NASHE, *Pierce Penilesse*, 1592

Drunkenness

Every country, city, town, village and other places hath abundance of alehouses, taverns and inns, which are so fraught with malt-worms, night and day, that you would wonder to see them. You shall have them there sitting at the wine and good-ale all the day long, yea, all the night too, peradventure a whole week together, so long as any money is left; swilling, gulling and carousing from one to another, till never a one can speak a ready word. Then, when with the spirit of the buttery they are thus possessed, a world it is to consider their gestures and demeanours, one towards another and towards every one else. How they stut and stammer, stagger and reel to and fro like madmen...and which is most horrible, some fall to swearing, cursing and banning, interlacing their speeches with curious terms of blasphemy, to the great dishonour of God, and offence of the godly ears present.

PHILIP STUBBES, *The Anatomie of Abuses*, 1583 (2nd ed.)

The sobriety of the English (two views)

Iago. Some wine, ho!
And let me the canakin clink, clink;
And let me the canakin clink:
A soldier's a man;
A life's but a span;
Why then let a soldier drink.
Some wine, boys!

Cassio. 'Fore God, an excellent song.

Iago. I learned it in England, where indeed they are most potent in potting; your Dane, your German, and your swag-bellied Hollander,—drink, ho!—are nothing to your English.

Othello, II. iii. 71–82

For the point of drinking, the English at the feast will drink two or three healths in remembrance of special friends, or respected honourable persons, and in our time some gentlemen and commanders from the wars of Netherland brought in the custom of the Germans' large carousing, but this custom is in our time also in good measure left. Likewise in some private gentlemen's houses, and with some captains and soldiers, and with the vulgar sort of citizens and artisans, large and intemperate drinking is used; but in general the greater and better part of the English hold all excess blameworthy, and drunkenness a reproachful vice. FYNES MORYSON, *Itinerary*, 1617

Shakespeare and Ben Jonson at the Mermaid Tavern

Many were the wit-combats betwixt him and Ben Jonson; which two I behold like a Spanish great

V. *An Elizabethan Stage*

galleon and an English man-of-war. Master Jonson (like the former) was built far higher in learning; solid, but slow, in his performances. Shakespeare, with the English man-of-war, lesser in bulk, but lighter in sailing, could turn with all tides, tack about, and take advantage of all winds, by the quickness of his wit and invention.

THOMAS FULLER, *English Worthies*, 1662

King James on the new fashion of tobacco smoking

How you are by this custom disabled in your goods, let the gentry of this land bear witness, some of them bestowing three, some four hundred pounds a year upon this precious stink, which I am sure might be bestowed upon many far better uses. I read indeed of a knavish courtier, who for abusing the favour of the emperor Alexander Severus, his master, by taking bribes to intercede for sundry persons in his master's ear (for whom he never once opened his mouth), was justly choked with smoke, with this doom, *Fumo pereat, qui fumum vendidit*: but of so many smoke-buyers, as are at this present in this kingdom, I never read nor heard.

And for the vanities committed in this filthy custom, is it not both great vanity and uncleanness, that at the table, a place of respect, of cleanliness, of modesty, men should not be ashamed to sit tossing of tobacco pipes, and puffing of the smoke of tobacco one to another, making the filthy smoke and stink thereof to exhale athwart the dishes, and infect the air, when very often men that abhor it are at their repast? Surely smoke becomes a kitchen far better than a dining chamber, and yet it makes a kitchen also oftentimes in the inward parts of men, soiling and infecting them, with an unctuous and oily kind of soot, as hath been found in some great tobacco takers, that after their death were opened.... The public use whereof, at all times and in all places, hath now so far prevailed, as divers men very sound both in judgment and complexion have been at last forced to take it also without desire, partly because they were ashamed to seem singular (like the two philosophers that were forced to duck themselves in that rain water, and so become fools as well as the rest of the people), and partly, to be as one that was content to eat garlic (which he did not love) that he might not be troubled with the smell of it in the breath of his fellows. And is it not a great vanity, that a man cannot heartily welcome his friend now, but straight they must be in hand with tobacco?

King James I, *A counter-blast to Tobacco*, 1672 (written 1604)

Barbers

Theodorus. What say you of the barbers and trimmers of men? are they so neat, and so fine fellows as they are said to be?

Amphilogus. There are no finer fellows under the sun, nor experter in their noble science of barbing than they be. And therefore in the fulness of their overflowing knowledge (oh ingenious heads, and worthy to be dignified with the diadem of folly and vain curiosity!) they have invented such strange fashions and monstrous manners of cuttings, trimmings, shavings and washings, that you would wonder to see. They have one manner of cut called the French cut, another the Spanish cut; one the Dutch cut, another the Italian; one the new cut, another the old; one of the bravado fashion, another of the mean fashion; one a gentleman's cut, another the common cut; one cut of the court, another of the country, with infinite the like varieties, which I overpass. They have also other kinds of cuts innumerable; and therefore when you come to be trimmed, they will ask you whether you will be cut to look terrible to your enemy, or amiable to your friend, grim and stern in countenance, or pleasant and demure (for they have divers kinds of cuts for all these purposes, or else they lie). Then, when they have done all their feats, it is a world to consider how their mustachios must be preserved and laid out, from one cheek to another, yea, almost from one ear to another, and turned up like two horns towards the forehead. Besides that, when they come to the cutting of the hair, what snipping and snapping of the scissors is there, what tricking and trimming, what rubbing, what scratching, what combing and clawing, what tricking and toying, and all to tawe out money, you may be sure. And when they come to washing, oh how gingerly they behave themselves therein. For then shall your mouth be bossed with the lather or foam that riseth off the balls (for they have their sweet balls wherewithal they use to wash); your eyes closed must be anointed therewith also. Then snap go the fingers, full bravely, God wot. Thus this tragedy ended, comes me warm cloths to wipe and dry him withal; next, the ears must be picked, and closed together again artificially forsooth; the hair of the nostrils cut away, and every thing done in order comely to behold.... You shall have also your orient perfumes for your nose, your fragrant waters for your face, wherewith you shall be all to besprinkled: your music again, and pleasant harmony, shall sound in your ears, and all to tickle the same with vain delight. And in the end your cloak shall be brushed, and "God be with you, gentleman!" PHILIP STUBBES, *Anatomie of Abuses* (Part ii), 1583

Fashionablé ladies

Hamlet (*to Yorick's skull*). Now get you to my lady's chamber, and tell her, let her paint an inch thick, to this favour she must come; make her laugh at that. *Hamlet*, v. i. 211–214

Look on beauty,
And you shall see 'tis purchas'd by the weight;
Which therein works a miracle in nature,
Making them lightest that wear most of it:

So are those crisped snaky golden locks
Which make such wanton gambols with the wind,
Upon supposed fairness, often known
To be the dowry of a second head,
The skull that bred them, in the sepulchre.

Merchant of Venice, III. ii. 88–96

Just to dinner they will arise, and after dinner go to bed again, and lie until supper. Yea, sometimes (by no sickness occasioned) they will lie in bed three days together: provided every morning before four o'clock they have their broths and their cullises, with pearl and gold sodden in them. If haply they break their hours and rise more early to go a-banquetting, they stand practising half a day with their looking-glasses, how to pierce and to glance and look alluringly amiable....

Their heads, with their top and top-gallant lawn baby-caps, and snow-resembled silver curlings, they make a plain puppet stage of....In their curious antic-woven garments they imitate and mock the worms and adders that must eat them. They shew the swellings of their mind, in the swellings and plumpings out of their apparel. Gorgeous ladies of the court, never was I admitted so near any of you, as to see how you torture poor old Time with sponging, pinning, and pouncing; but they say his sickle you have burst in twain, to make your periwigs more elevated arches of.

THOMAS NASHE, *Christs Teares over Ierusalem*, 1593

Lap-dogs

The third sort of dogs of the gentle kind is the spaniel gentle, or comforter, or (as the common term is) the fisting-hound, and those are called Melitei, of the Island Malta, from whence they were brought hither. These are little and pretty, proper and fine, and sought out far and near to satisfy the nice delicacy of dainty dames, and wanton women's wills; instruments of folly to play and dally withal, in trifling away the treasure of time, to withdraw their minds from more commendable exercises,...a silly poor shift to shun their irksome idleness. These sybaritical puppies, the smaller they be (and thereto if they have an hole in the foreparts of their heads) the better they are accepted, the more pleasure also they provoke, as meet playfellows for mincing mistresses to bear in their bosoms, to keep company withal in their chambers, to succour with sleep in bed, and nourish with meat at board, to lie in their laps, and lick their lips, as they lie (like young Dianas) in their waggons and coaches....Yea, they oft feed them of the best, where the poor man's child at their doors can hardly come by the worst.

WILLIAM HARRISON, *Description of England*, 1587 (2nd ed.)

The plague

In Shakespeare's day the plague was an annual visitor to London. When there were over 30 deaths a week the theatres were closed. There were very few summers in which this did not happen.

Civis. Good wife, the daily jangling and ringing of the bells, the coming in of the minister to every house in ministering the communion, in reading the homily of death, the digging up of graves, the sparring in of windows, and the blazing forth of the blue cross, do make my heart tremble and quake. Alas, what shall I do to save my life?

Uxor. Sir, we are but young, and have but a time in this world, what doth it profit us to gather riches together, and can not enjoy them? Why tarry we here so long? I do think every hour a year until we be gone; my heart is as cold as a stone, and as heavy as lead, God help me. Seeing that we have sent our children forth three weeks past into a good air and a sweet country, let us follow them. We shall be welcome to your brother's house, I dare say; my sister will rejoice in our coming, and so will all our friends there. Let us take leave of our neighbours, and return merely home again when the plague is past, and the dog days ended; and there you may occupy your stock, and have gain thereof.

William Bullein, *A Dialogue against the Pestilence*, 1573 (1st ed. 1564)

§ 4. THE THEATRE

An allusion in 1592 by Robert Greene, the well-known dramatist of the older school of "university wits", to a certain "upstart crow, beautified with our feathers", who "is in his own conceit the only Shake-scene in a country", shews that by this year Shakespeare had already become prominent both as player and playwright. And in 1594 we find him named as one of the chief actors in the Lord Chamberlain's company, who played that Christmas before the Queen. At King James's accession his company became the King's Men and he ranked as a Groom of the Chamber.

Duke. This wide and universal theatre
Presents more woeful pageants than the scene
Wherein we play in.
Jaques. All the world's a stage,
And all the men and women merely players:
They have their exits and their entrances;
And one man in his time plays many parts,
His acts being seven ages.

As You Like It, II. vii. 137–143

Life's but a walking shadow, a poor player
That struts and frets his hour upon the stage,
And then is heard no more. *Macbeth*, V. v. 24–26

A German describes English theatres and bear-gardens

Without the city are some theatres, where English actors represent almost every day comedies and tragedies to very numerous audiences; these are concluded with variety of dances, accompanied by excellent music and the excessive applause of those that are present. Not far from one of these theatres,

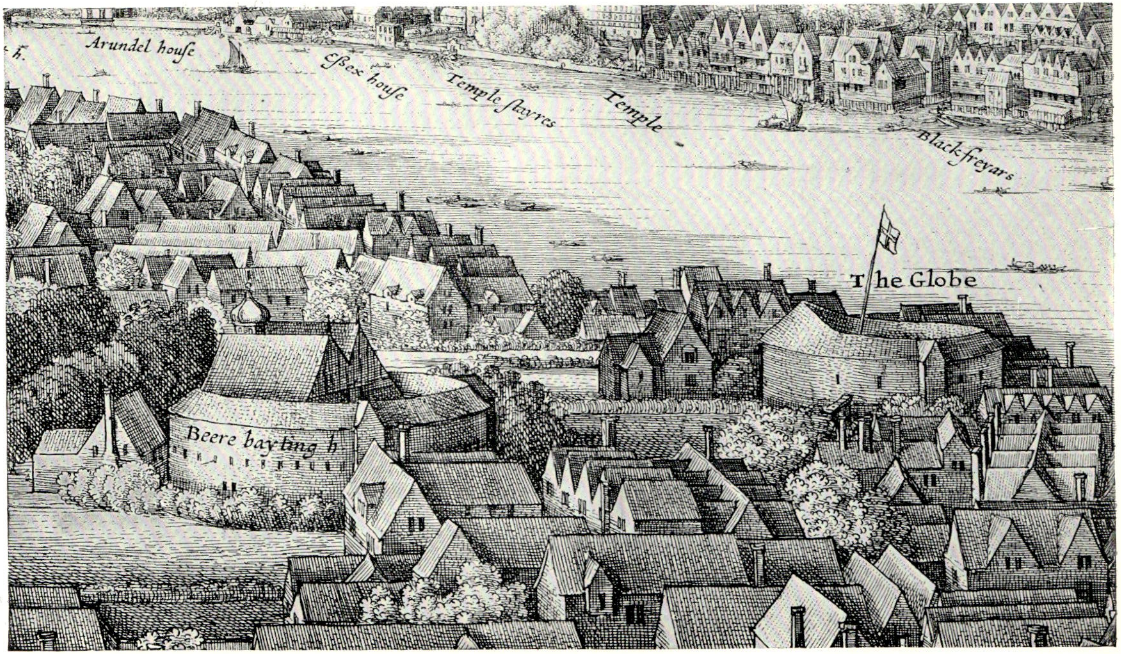

VI. *The Globe Theatre, and a Bear-garden, Bankside*

which are all built of wood, lies the royal barge, close to the river Thames. It has two splendid cabins, beautifully ornamented with glass windows, painting and gilding; it is kept upon dry ground, and sheltered from the weather.

There is still another place, built in the form of a theatre, which serves for the baiting of bears and bulls. They are fastened behind, and then worried by those great English dogs and mastiffs, but not without great risk to the dogs from the teeth of the one and the horns of the other; and it sometimes happens they are killed upon the spot. Fresh ones are immediately supplied in the places of those that are wounded or tired. . . . At these spectacles and everywhere else, the English are constantly smoking the Nicotian weed which in America is called *Tobaca*—others call it *Paetum*—and generally in this manner: they have pipes on purpose made of clay, into the farther end of which they put the herb, so dry that it may be rubbed into powder, and lighting it, they draw the smoke into their mouths, which they puff out again through their nostrils, like funnels, along with it plenty of phlegm and defluxion from the head. In these theatres, fruits, such as apples, pears and nuts, according to the season, are carried about to be sold, as well as wine and ale.

PAUL HENTZNER, *Travels in England*, 1598 [Rye]

English and Italian theatres compared by an Englishman in Venice

I was at one of their play-houses, where I saw a comedy acted. The house is very beggarly and base in comparison of our stately play-houses in England: neither can their actors compare with us for apparel, shews and music. Here I observed certain things that I never saw before. For I saw women act, a thing that I never saw before, though I have heard that it hath been sometimes used in London; and they performed it with as good a grace, action, gesture and whatsoever convenient for a player, as ever I saw any masculine actor.

THOMAS CORYAT, *Crudities*, 1611

Shakespeare on acting

Hamlet. Speak the speech, I pray you, as I pronounced it to you, trippingly on the tongue; but if you mouth it, as many of your players do, I had as lief the town-crier spoke my lines. Nor do not saw the air too much with your hand, thus; but use all gently: for in the very torrent, tempest, and—as I may say—whirlwind of passion, you must acquire and beget a temperance, that may give it smoothness. O! it offends me to the soul to hear a robustious periwig-pated fellow tear a passion to tatters, to very rags, to split the ears of the groundlings, who for the most part are capable of nothing but inexplicable dumb-shows and noise: I would have such a fellow whipped for o'er-doing Termagant; it out-herods Herod: pray you, avoid it.

First Player. I warrant your honour.

Hamlet. Be not too tame neither, but let your own discretion be your tutor: suit the action to the word, the word to the action; with this special observance, that you o'erstep not the modesty of nature; for anything so overdone is from the purpose of playing, whose end, both at the first and now, was and is, to hold, as 'twere, the mirror up to nature; to show virtue her own feature, scorn her own image, and the very age and body of the time his form and pressure. Now, this overdone, or come tardy off, though it make the unskilful laugh, cannot but make the judicious grieve; the censure of which one must in your allowance o'erweigh a whole theatre of others. O! there be players that I have seen play, and heard others praise, and that highly, not to speak it profanely, that, neither having the accent of Christians nor the gait of Christian, pagan, nor man, have so strutted and bellowed that I have thought some of nature's journeymen had made men and not made them well, they imitated humanity so abominably.

First Player. I hope we have reformed that indifferently with us.

Hamlet. O! reform it altogether. And let those that play your clowns speak no more than is set down for them; for there be of them that will themselves laugh, to set on some quantity of barren spectators to laugh too, though in the mean time some necessary question of the play be then to be considered; that's villainous, and shows a most pitiful ambition in the fool that uses it. *Hamlet*, III. ii. 1–50

A story of Richard Tarlton, a great comic actor

Amongst other choleric wise justices he was one, that having a play presented before him and his township by Tarlton and the rest of his fellows, her Majesty's servants, and they were now entering into their first merriment (as they call it), the people began exceedingly to laugh when Tarlton first peeped out his head. Whereat the justice, not a little moved, and seeing with his becks and nods he could not make them cease, he went with his staff, and beat them round about unmercifully on the bare pates, in that they, being but farmers and poor country hinds, would presume to laugh at the Queen's men, and make no more account of her cloth in his presence. THOMAS NASHE, *Pierce Penilesse*, 1592

A royal licence for Shakespeare's company, "The King's Players," May 19, 1603

James by the grace of God etc. To all justices, mayors, sheriffs, constables, headboroughs and other our officers and loving subjects greeting. Know ye that We of our special grace, certain knowledge and mere motion, have licensed and authorised and by these presents do license and authorise these our servants Lawrence Fletcher, William Shakespeare, Richard Burbage, Augustine Phillipps, John Heming, Henry Condell, William Sly, Robert Armin, Richard Cowley, and the rest of their associates freely to use and exercise the art and faculty of playing comedies, tragedies, histories, interludes, morals, pastorals, stage-plays, and such others like as they have already studied or hereafter shall use or study, as well for the recreation of our loving subjects as for our solace and pleasure when we shall think good to see them during our pleasure. And the said comedies, tragedies, histories, interludes, morals, pastorals, stage-plays and such like to shew and exercise publicly to their best commodity, when the infection of the plague shall decrease, as well within their now usual house, called the Globe, within our county of Surrey, as also within any town-halls or moot-halls or other convenient places within the liberties and freedom of any other city, university town or borough whatsoever within our said realms and dominions. Willing and commanding you and every [one] of you as you tender our pleasure not only to permit and suffer them herein without any your lets and hindrances or molestations during our said pleasure, but also to be aiding and assisting to them if any wrong be to them offered. And to allow them such former courtesies as hath been given to men of their place and quality, and also what further favour you shall show to these our servants, for our sake, we shall take kindly at your hands. In witness whereof etc. witness ourself at Westminster the nineteenth day of May.

PURITAN OPPOSITION TO THE THEATRE

From the erection of the theatres in 1576 to their suppression at the outbreak of the Civil War, the Puritan party waged an unceasing warfare against the stage. But for the protection of the court the Elizabethan drama would have come to an untimely end before Shakespeare reached London. The tracts on either side of the controversy tell us a good deal about the theatrical and dramatic conditions of the day.

Puritan denunciation from Paul's Cross

Look but upon the common plays in London, and see the multitude that flocketh to them and followeth them. Behold the sumptuous theatre houses, a continual monument of London's prodigality and folly. But I understand they are now forbidden because of the plague. I like the policy well if it hold still, for a disease is but lodged or patched up that is not cured in the cause, and the cause of plagues is sin, if you look to it well: and the cause of sin are plays: therefore the cause of plagues are plays.

Will not a filthy play, with the blast of a trumpet, sooner call thither a thousand, than an hour's tolling of a bell bring to the sermon a hundred? Nay even here in the city, without it be at this place and some other certain ordinary audience, where shall you find a reasonable company? Whereas if you resort to the Theater, the Curtain, and other places of plays in the city, you shall on the Lord's day have those places, with many other that I cannot reckon, so full as possible they can throng, besides a great number of other lets to pull from the hearing of the word of which I will speak hereafter. . . . What [=why] should I speak of beastly plays, against which out of this place every man crieth out? Have we not houses of purpose built with great charges for the maintenance of them? and that without the liberties, as who would say: "There, let them say what they will, we will play." I know not how I might with the godly learned especially more discommend the gorgeous playing-place erected in the fields than to term it, as they please to have it called, a Theater, that is even after the manner of the old heathenish theatre at Rome, a shew-place of all beastly and filthy matters, to the which it cannot be chosen that men should resort without learning thence much corruption. . . For reckoning with the least, the gain that is reaped of eight ordinary places in the city, which I know, by playing but once a week (whereas many times they play twice or sometimes thrice) it amounteth to two thousand pounds by the year.

From *A Sermon Preached at Paules Crosse*, 1578

§ 5. THE COURT

What infinite heart's ease
Must kings neglect that private men enjoy!
And what have kings that privates have not too,
Save ceremony, save general ceremony?
And what art thou, thou idle ceremony?
What kind of god art thou, that suffer'st more
Of mortal griefs than do thy worshippers?
What are thy rents? what are thy comings-in?

* * * * *

'Tis not the balm, the sceptre and the ball,
The sword, the mace, the crown imperial,
The intertissued robe of gold and pearl,
The farced title running 'fore the king,
The throne he sits on, nor the tide of pomp
That beats upon the high shore of this world,
No, not all these, thrice-gorgeous ceremony,
Not all these, laid in bed majestical,
Can sleep so soundly as the wretched slave,
Who with a body fill'd and vacant mind
Gets him to rest, cramm'd with distressful bread.

Henry V, IV. i. 256–290

Queen Elizabeth at Greenwich (by a German visitor)

Elizabeth, the reigning Queen of England, was born at the royal palace of Greenwich, and here she generally resides, particularly in summer, for the delightfulness of its situation. We were admitted by an order, which Mr Rogers had procured from the Lord Chamberlain, into the presence-chamber hung with rich tapestry, and the floor, after the English fashion, strewed with hay, through which the Queen

VII. *Queen Elizabeth as Patron of Letters*

commonly passes on her way to chapel. At the door stood a gentleman dressed in velvet, with a gold chain, whose office was to introduce to the Queen any person of distinction that came to wait on her. It was Sunday, when there is usually the greatest attendance of nobility. In the same hall were the Archbishop of Canterbury, the Bishop of London, a great number of counsellors of state, officers of the crown, and gentlemen, who waited the Queen's coming out, which she did from her own apartment when it was time to go to prayers, attended in the following manner:—

First went gentlemen, barons, earls, knights of the Garter, all richly dressed and bareheaded; next came the Lord High Chancellor of England, bearing the seals in a red silk purse, between two, one of whom carried the royal sceptre, the other the sword of state in a red scabbard, studded with golden fleur-de-lis, the point upwards; next came the Queen, in the 65th year of her age (as we were told), very majestic; her face oblong, fair but wrinkled; her eyes small, yet black and pleasant; her nose a little hooked, her lips narrow, and her teeth black (a defect the English seem subject to, from their too great use of sugar); she had in her ears two pearls with very rich drops; her hair was of an auburn colour, but false; upon her head she had a small crown, reported to be made of some of the gold of the celebrated Luneburg table; her bosom was uncovered, as all the English ladies have it till they marry; and she had on a necklace of exceeding fine jewels; her hands were slender, her fingers rather long, and her stature neither tall nor low; her air was stately, her manner of speaking mild and obliging. That day she was dressed in white silk, bordered with pearls of the size of beans, and over it a mantle of black silk shot with silver threads; her train was very long, the end of it borne by a marchioness; instead of a chain, she had an oblong collar of gold and jewels. As she went along in all this state and magnificence, she spoke very graciously, first to one, then to another (whether foreign ministers, or those who attend for different reasons), in English, French and Italian; for besides being well skilled in Greek, Latin and the languages I have mentioned, she is mistress of Spanish, Scotch and Dutch. Whoever speaks to her, it is kneeling; now and then she raises some with her hand. While wc were there, William Slawata, a Bohemian baron, had letters to present to her; and she, after pulling off her glove, gave him her right hand to kiss, sparkling with rings and jewels—a mark of particular favour. Wherever she turned her face as she was going along, everybody fell down on their knees. The ladies of the court followed next to her, very handsome and well-shaped, and for the most part dressed in white. She was guarded on each side by the gentlemen pensioners, fifty in number, with gilt halberds. In the antechapel, next the hall where we were, petitions were presented to her, and she received them most graciously, which occasioned the acclamation of *God save the Quene Elizabeth!* She answered it with *I thancke you myn good peupel.* In the chapel was excellent music; as soon as it and the service were over, which scarcely exceeded half-an-hour, the Queen returned in the same state and order, and prepared to go to dinner. But while she was still at prayers, we saw her table set out with the following solemnity:—

A gentleman entered the room bearing a rod, and along with him another who had a table-cloth, which after they had both knelt three times, with the utmost veneration, he spread upon the table, and after kneeling again they both retired. Then came two others, one with the rod again, the other with a salt-cellar, a plate and bread; when they had knelt as the others had done, and placed what was brought upon the table, they too retired with the same ceremonies performed by the first. At last came an unmarried lady of extraordinary beauty (we were told that she was a countess) and along with her a married one, bearing a tasting-knife; the former was dressed in white silk, who, when she had prostrated herself three times, in the most graceful manner, approached the table and rubbed the plates with bread and salt with as much awe as if the Queen had been present. When they had waited there a little while, the yeomen of the guard entered, bareheaded, clothed in scarlet, with a golden rose upon their backs, bringing in at each turn a course of twenty-four dishes, served in silver, most of it gilt; these dishes were received by a gentleman in the same order as they were brought and placed upon the table, while the lady-taster gave to each of the guard a mouthful to eat of the particular dish he had brought, for fear of any poison. During the time that this guard, which consists of the tallest and stoutest men that can be found in all England, 100 in number, being carefully selected for this service, were bringing dinner, twelve trumpets and two kettle-drums made the hall ring for half-an-hour together. At the end of all this ceremonial, a number of unmarried ladies appeared, who with particular solemnity lifted the meat off the table, and conveyed it into the Queen's inner and more private chamber, where after she had chosen for herself, the rest goes to the ladies of the court. The Queen dines and sups alone with very few attendants; and it is very seldom that any body, foreigner or native, is admitted at that time, and then only at the intercession of some distinguished personage.

PAUL HENTZNER, *Travels in England*, 1598 [Rye]

The Courtier

The courtier's, soldier's, scholar's eye, tongue, sword,
The expectancy and rose of the fair state,
The glass of fashion and the mould of form,
The observed of all observers. *Hamlet*, III. i. 160–163

To ride comely, to run fair at the tilt or ring, to play at all weapons, to shoot fair in bow or surely in gun, to vault lustily, to run, to leap, to wrestle, to swim, to dance comely, to sing and play of instruments cunningly, to hawk, to hunt, to play at tennis and all pastimes generally which be joined with labour, used in open place and on the daylight, containing either some fit exercise for war or some pleasant pastime for peace, be not only comely and decent, but also very necessary, for a courtly gentleman to use....

Take heed therefore, ye great ones in the court, yea, though ye be the greatest of all, take heed what ye do, take heed how ye live. For as you great ones use to do, so all mean men love to do. You be indeed makers or marrers of all men's manners within the realm. For though God hath placed you to be chief in making of laws, to bear greatest authority, to command all others, yet God doth order that all your laws, all your authority, all your commandments, do not half so much with mean men, as doth your example and manner of living.

ROGER ASCHAM, *The Scholemaster*, 1570

Touchstone as a Courtier

Jaques. Good my lord, bid him welcome. This is the motley-minded gentleman that I have so often met in the forest: he hath been a courtier, he swears.

Touchstone. If any man doubt that, let him put me to my purgation. I have trod a measure; I have flattered a lady; I have been politic with my friend, smooth with mine enemy; I have undone three tailors; I have had four quarrels, and like to have fought one.

Jaques. And how was that ta'en up?

Touchstone. Faith, we met, and found the quarrel was upon the seventh cause.

Jaques. How seventh cause?...How did you find the quarrel on the seventh cause?

Touchstone. Upon a lie seven times removed...as thus, sir. I did dislike the cut of a certain courtier's beard: he sent me word, if I said his beard was not cut well, he was in the mind it was: this is called the "retort courteous." If I sent him word again, it was not well cut, he would send me word, he cut it to please himself: this is called the "quip modest." If again, it was not well cut, he disabled my judgment: this is called the "reply churlish." If again, it was not cut well, he would answer, I spake not true: this is called the "reproof valiant": if again, it was not well cut, he would say, I lie: this is called the "countercheck quarrelsome": and so to the "lie circumstantial" and the "lie direct."

Jaques. And how oft did you say his beard was not well cut?

Touchstone. I durst go no further than the "lie circumstantial," nor he durst not give me the "lie direct"; and so we measured swords and parted.

Jaques. Can you nominate in order now the degrees of the lie?

Touchstone. O sir, we quarrel in print; by the book, as you have books for good manners: I will name you the degrees. The first, the "retort courteous"; the second, the "quip modest"; the third, the "reply churlish"; the fourth, the "reproof valiant"; the fifth, the "countercheck quarrelsome"; the sixth, the "lie with circumstance"; the seventh, the "lie direct." All these you may avoid but the lie direct; and you may avoid that too with an "if." I knew when seven justices could not take up a quarrel; but when the parties were met themselves, one of them thought but of an "if," as "If you said so, then I said so"; and they shook hands, and swore brothers. Your "if" is the only peace-maker; much virtue in "if."

As You Like It, v. iv. 40–109

Masques at Court

Duke Theseus. Come now; what masques, what dances shall we have,
To wear away this long age of three hours
Between our after-supper and bed-time?
Where is our usual manager of mirth?
What revels are in hand?

A Midsummer Night's Dream, v. i. 32–36

Procession of masquers, in honour of the marriage of Princess Elizabeth, daughter of James I., Feb. 11–16, 1613

Upon Shrove Monday at night, the gentlemen of the Middle Temple and Lincoln's Inn, with their train for this business, assembled in Chancery Lane, at the house of Sir Edward Philips, Master of the Rolls, and about eight of the clock they marched thence through the Strand, to the court at Whitehall, in this manner. First rode fifty choice gentlemen richly attired, and as gallantly mounted, with every one his footman to attend him; these rode very stately like a vanguard. Next after, with fit distance, marched an antic or mock-masque of baboons, attired like fantastic travellers in very strange and confused manner, riding upon asses or dwarf jades, using all apish and mocking tricks to the people, moving much laughter as they passed with torches on either side to shew their state to be as ridiculous as the rest was noble. After them came two chariots triumphal, very pleasant and full of state, wherein rode the choice musicians of this kingdom, in robes like to the Virginian priests, with sundry devices, all pleasant and significant, with two ranks of torches. Then came the chief masquers with great state in white Indian habit or like the great princes of Barbary, richly embroidered with the golden sun, with suitable ornaments in all points; about their

VIII. *An Elizabethan Country House*

necks were ruffs of feathers, spangled and beset with pearl and silver, and upon their heads lofty coronets suitable to the rest. They wore long silk stockings, curiously embroidered with gold to the mid-leg. Their buskins were likewise embroidered, and in their hands, as they rode, they brandished cane darts of the finest gold: their vizards were of olive colour, their hair long and black, down to their shoulders. The horses for rich show equalled the masquers: their caparisons were enchased with suns of gold and ornamental jewels, with silver scarfing over the whole caparison and about their heads, which made such a strange and glorious show, that it dazzled the eyes of the beholders with great admiration. Every of these horses had two Moors to attend them, attired like Indian slaves, with wreaths of gold and watshod about their heads, being about an hundred in number. The torch-bearers carried torches of virgin wax, the staves whereof were great canes gilded all over, and their habits were likewise of the Indian garb, but more extravagant than those of the masquers. The masquers rode single, and had every man his torch-bearer riding before him. All which, with the last triumphal chariot, wherein sat many strange attired personages, with their emblems, conceitful and variable devices, made a wondrous pleasing show. And thus they marched through the Strand to Whitehall, where the King, the Prince, the bride and bridegroom, and the chief nobility stood in the gallery before the tilt-yard to behold their approach; and because there should be a full view had of their state and train, the King caused them to march one turn about the list; and being dismounted, they were honourably attended through the gallery to a chamber, in which they were to make them ready for performance of their scene in the hall; in which place were erected their sundry properties and devices, formerly mentioned, where they performed all things answerable to the best of expectation, and received as royal thanks and commendations.

EDMOND HOWES, *Annales*, 1615

IV

HOME AGAIN

In 1597 Shakespeare, successful as actor and dramatist, begins to turn his thoughts towards home. In that year he buys New Place, the largest house in Stratford, and other property in the town. About 1608 he probably took up his residence there more or less permanently; and in 1611 or thereabouts he retired altogether from the stage. Perhaps his latest plays were written wholly or in part in the country.

Houses and Furniture

My house within the city
Is richly furnished with plate and gold:
Basins and ewers to lave her dainty hands;
My hangings all of Tyrian tapestry;
In ivory coffers I have stuff'd my crowns;
In cypress chests my arras counterpoints,
Costly apparel, tents, and canopies,
Fine linen, Turkey cushions boss'd with pearl,
Valance of Venice gold in needle-work,
Pewter and brass, and all things that belong
To house or housekeeping: then at my farm
I have a hundred milch-kine to the pail,
Six score fat oxen standing in my stalls,
And all things answerable to this portion.

Taming of the Shrew, II. i. 340–353

The greatest part of our building in the cities and good towns of England consisteth only of timber, for as yet few of the houses of the communalty (except here and there in the west-country towns) are made of stone, although they may in my opinion in divers other places be builded so good cheap of the one as of the other. In old time the houses of the Britons were slightly set up with a few posts and many raddles, with stable and all offices under one roof, the like whereof almost is to be seen in the fenny countries and northern parts unto this day, where for lack of wood they are enforced to continue this ancient manner of building....

Certes this rude kind of building made the Spaniards in Queen Mary's days to wonder, but chiefly when they saw what large diet was used in many of these so homely cottages; insomuch that one of no small reputation amongst them said after this manner—"These English," quoth he, "have their houses made of sticks and dirt, but they fare commonly so well as the king." Whereby it appeareth that he liked better of our good fare in such coarse cabins than of their own thin diet in their princelike habitations and palaces. In like sort as every country house is thus apparelled on the outside, so is it inwardly divided into sundry rooms above and beneath; and, where plenty of wood is, they cover them with tiles, otherwise with straw, sedge or reed, except some quarry of slate be near hand, from whence they have for their money much as may suffice them. The clay wherewith our houses are impanelled is either white, red or blue; and of these the first doth participate very much of the nature of our chalk, the second is called loam, but the third eftsoons changeth colour as soon as it is wrought, notwithstanding that it looks blue when it is thrown out of the pit....

The walls of our houses on the inner sides in like sort be either hanged with tapestry, arras work, or painted cloths, wherein either divers histories, or herbs, beasts, knots and such like are stained, or else they are ceiled with oak of our own, or wainscot brought hither out of the east countries, whereby the rooms are not a little commended, made warm and much more close than otherwise they would be. As for stoves, we have not hitherto used them greatly, yet do they now begin to be made in divers houses of the gentry and wealthy citizens, who build them not to work and feed in, as in Germany and elsewhere, but now and then to sweat in, as occasion and need shall require it....

The furniture of our houses also exceedeth, and is grown in manner even to passing delicacy: and herein I do not speak of the nobility and gentry only, but likewise of the lowest sort in most places of our south country that have anything at all to take to. Certes in noblemen's houses it is not rare to see abundance of arras, rich hangings of tapestry, silver vessels, and so much other plate as may furnish sundry cupboards to the sum oftentimes of a thousand or two thousand pounds at the least, whereby the value of this and the rest of their stuff doth grow to be almost inestimable. Likewise in the houses of knights, gentlemen, merchantmen, and some other wealthy citizens, it is not geason to behold generally their great provision of tapestry, Turkey work, pewter, brass, fine linen, and thereto costly cupboards of plate, worth five or six hundred or a thousand pounds to be deemed by estimation. But, as herein all these sorts do far exceed their elders and predecessors, and in neatness and curiosity the merchant all other, so in time past the costly furniture stayed there, whereas now it is descended yet lower even unto the inferior artificers and many farmers, who, by virtue of their old and not of their new leases, have for the most part learned also to garnish their cupboards with plate, their joined beds with tapestry and silk hangings, and their tables with carpets and fine napery, whereby the wealth of our country (God be praised therefore, and give us grace to employ it well) doth infinitely appear.

WILLIAM HARRISON, *Description of England*, 1587 (2nd ed.)

Housekeeping and the table

Let me see; what am I to buy for our sheep-shearing feast? "Three pound of sugar; five pound of currants; rice," what will this sister of mine do with rice?. . . I must have saffron, to colour the warden pies; mace, dates,—none; that's out of my note: nutmegs seven; a race or two of ginger,—but that I may beg,—four pound of prunes, and as many of raisins o' the sun.

The Winter's Tale, IV. ii. 38–53

An English Housewife

Next unto sanctity and holiness of life, it is meet that our English housewife be a woman of great modesty and temperance as well inwardly as outwardly. Inwardly, as in her behaviour and carriage towards her husband, wherein she shall shun all violence of rage, passion and humour, coveting less to direct than to be directed, appearing ever unto him pleasant, amiable and delightful; and though occasion, mishaps or the misgovernment of his will may induce her to contrary thoughts, yet virtuously to suppress them, and with a mild sufferance rather to call him home from his error, than with the strength of anger to abate the least spark of his evil, calling into her mind that evil and uncomely language is deformed though uttered even to servants, but most monstrous and ugly when it appears before the presence of a husband. Outwardly, as in her apparel and diet, both which she shall proportion according to the competency of her husband's estate and calling, making her circle rather strait than large, for it is a rule if we extend to the uttermost we take away increase, if we go a hair breadth beyond we enter into consumption, but if we preserve any part, we build strong forts against the adversaries of fortune, provided that such preservation be honest and conscionable: for as lavish prodigality is brutish, so miserable covetousness is hellish. Let therefore the housewife's garments be comely, cleanly and strong, made as well to preserve the health, as adorn the person, altogether without toyish garnishes or the gloss of light colours, and as far from the vanity of new and fantastic fashions, as near to the comely imitations of modest matrons. Let her diet be wholesome and cleanly, prepared at due hours, and cooked with care and diligence; let it be rather to satisfy nature than our affections, and apter to kill hunger than revive new appetites; let it proceed more from the provision of her own yard, than the furniture of the markets; and let it be rather esteemed for the familiar acquaintance she hath with it, than for the strangeness and rarity it bringeth from other countries.

To conclude, our English housewife must be of chaste thought, stout courage, patient, untired, watchful, diligent, witty, pleasant, constant in friendship, full of good neighbourhood, wise in discourse, but not frequent therein, sharp and quick of speech, but not bitter or talkative, secret in her affairs, comfortable in her counsels, and generally skilful in all the worthy knowledges which do belong to her vocation. GERVASE MARKHAM, *The English Hus-wife*, 1615

Of the food and diet of the English

In number of dishes and change of meat the nobility of England (whose cooks are for the most part musical-headed Frenchmen and strangers) do most exceed, sith there is no day in manner that passeth over their heads wherein they have not only beef, mutton, veal, lamb, kid, pork, cony, capon, pig or so many of these as the season yieldeth, but also some portion of the red or fallow deer, beside great variety of fish and wild-fowl, and thereto sundry other delicates wherein the sweet hand of the seafaring Portingal is not wanting: so that for a man to dine with one of them, and to taste of every dish that standeth before him (which few use to do, but each one feedeth upon that meat him best liketh for the time...) is rather to yield unto a conspiracy with a great deal of meat for the speedy suppression of natural health, than the use of a necessary mean to satisfy himself with a competent repast to sustain his body withal....

As for drink it is usually filled in pots, goblets, jugs, bowls of silver, in noblemen's houses; also in fine Venice glasses of all forms; and, for want of these elsewhere, in pots of earth of sundry colours and moulds, whereof many are garnished with silver, or at the leastwise in pewter, all which notwithstanding are seldom set on the table, but each one, as necessity urgeth, calleth for a cup of such drink as him listeth to have, so that, when he hath tasted of it, he delivereth the cup again to some one of the standers by, who, making it clean by pouring out the drink that remaineth, restoreth it to the cupboard from whence he fetched the same....

Heretofore there hath been much more time spent

in eating and drinking than commonly is in these days; for whereas of old we had breakfasts in the forenoon, beverages or nunchions after dinner, and thereto rear-suppers generally when it was time to go to rest. . . now these odd repasts, thanked be God, are very well left, and each one in manner (except here and there some young hungry stomach that cannot fast till dinner-time) contenteth himself with dinner and supper only. . . .

With us the nobility, gentry and students do ordinarily go to dinner at eleven before noon, and to supper at five or between five and six at afternoon. The merchants dine and sup seldom before twelve at noon, and six at night, especially in London. The husbandmen dine also at high noon as they call it, and sup at seven or eight; but out of the term in our universities the scholars dine at ten. As for the poorest sort they generally dine and sup when they may, so that to talk of their order of repast it were but a needless matter.

WILLIAM HARRISON, *Description of England*, 1587 (2nd ed.)

Forks

Here I will mention a thing that might have been spoken of before, in discourse of the first Italian town. I observed a custom in all those Italian cities and towns through the which I passed, that is not used in any other country that I saw in my travels, neither do I think that any other nation of Christendom doth use it, but only Italy. The Italians, and also most strangers that are commorant in Italy, do always at their meals use a little fork when they cut their meat. For while with their knife, which they hold in one hand, they cut the meat out of the dish, they fasten their fork which they hold in their other hand upon the same dish, so that whatsoever he be that, sitting in the company of any others at meal, should unadvisedly touch the dish of meat with his fingers from which all at the table do cut, he will give occasion of offence unto the company, as having transgressed the laws of good manners, in so much that for his error he shall be at the least brow-beaten if not reprehended in words. This form of feeding I understand is generally used in all places of Italy, their forks being for the most part made of iron or steel, and some of silver, but those are used only by gentlemen. The reason of this their curiosity is, because the Italian cannot by any means endure to have his dish touched with fingers, seeing all men's fingers are not alike clean. Hereupon I myself thought good to imitate the Italian fashion by this forked cutting of meat, not only while I was in Italy, but also in Germany, and oftentimes in England since I came home: being once quipped for that frequent using of my fork by a certain learned gentleman, a familiar friend of mine, one Mr Laurence Whitaker, who in his merry humour doubted not to call me at table *furcifer*, only for using a fork at feeding, but for no other cause.

THOMAS CORYAT, *Crudities*, 1611

The Ideal Cook

It resteth now that I proceed unto cookery itself, which is the dressing and ordering of meat in good and wholesome manner; to which, when our housewife shall address herself, she shall well understand that these qualities must ever accompany it: first, she must be cleanly both in body and garments, she must have a quick eye, a curious nose, a perfect taste and a ready ear. She must not be butter-fingered, sweet-toothed nor faint-hearted; for the first will let everything fall, the second will consume what it should increase, and the last will lose time with too much niceness.

GERVASE MARKHAM, *The English Hus-wife*, 1615

Recipe for an Elizabethan mince-pie

Take a leg of mutton, and cut the best of the best flesh from the bone, and parboil it well: then put to it three pound of the best mutton suet, and shred it very small: then spread it abroad, and season it with pepper and salt, cloves and mace: then put in good store of currants, great raisins and prunes, clean washed and picked, a few dates sliced, and some orange-pills sliced: then being all well mixed together, put it into a coffin, or into divers coffins, and so bake them: and when they are served up, open the lids, and strew store of sugar on the top of the meat, and upon the lid. And in this sort you may also bake beef or veal; only the beef would not be parboiled, and the veal will ask a double quantity of suet.

GERVASE MARKHAM, *The English Hus-wife*, 1623 (2nd ed.)

Going to bed (a doctor's advice)

To bedward be you merry or have merry company about you, so that to bedward no anger nor heaviness, sorrow nor pensivefulness, do trouble or disquiet you. To bedward and also in the morning, use to have a fire in your chamber, to waste and consume the evil vapours within the chamber, for the breath of man may putrefy the air within the chamber: I do advertise you not to stand nor to sit by the fire, but stand or sit a good way off from the fire, taking the flavour of it, for fire doth arify and doth dry up a man's blood, and doth make stark the sinews and joints of man. In the night let the windows of your house, specially of your chamber, be closed. When you be in your bed, lie a little while on your left side, and sleep on your right side....

Let your nightcap be of scarlet, and this, I do advertise you, to cause to be made [of] a good thick quilt of cotton, or else of pure flocks or of clean wool, and let the covering of it be of white fustian, and lay it on the featherbed that you do lie on; and in your bed lie not too hot nor too cold, but in a temperance. Old ancient doctors of physic saith eight hours of sleep in summer and nine in winter is sufficient for any man; but I do think the sleep ought to be taken as the complexion of man is. When you do rise in the morning, rise with mirth and remember God. Let your hosen be brushed within and without, and flavour the inside of them against the fire; use linen socks, or linen hosen next your legs: when you be out of your bed, stretch forth your legs and arms and your body, cough and spit....

ANDREW BOORDE, *A Compendyous Regyment or a Dietary of helth*, 1542

CONCLUSION

AN ELIZABETHAN DAY

And then he drew a dial from his poke,
And, looking on it with lack-lustre eye,
Says very wisely, "It is ten o'clock;
Thus may we see," quoth he, "how the world wags:
'Tis but an hour ago since it was nine,
And after one hour more 'twill be eleven;
And so, from hour to hour we ripe and ripe,
And then from hour to hour we rot and rot,
And thereby hangs a tale."

As You Like It, II. vii. 20–28

One of the Clock

It is now the first hour and time is, as it were, stepping out of darkness and stealing towards the day: the cock calls to his hen and bids her beware of the fox, and the watch, having walked the streets, take a nap upon a stall: the bell-man calls to the maids to look to their locks, their fire and their light, and the child in the cradle calls to the nurse. . . the cat sits watching behind the cupboard for a mouse, and the flea sucks on sweet flesh, till he is ready to burst with blood: the spirits of the studious start out of their dreams, and if they cannot fall asleep again, then to the book and the wax candle: the dog at the door frays the thief from the house, and the thief within the house may hap to be about his business. In some places bells are rung to certain orders: but the quiet sleeper never tells the clock. Not to dwell too long upon it, I hold it the farewell of the night and the forerunner to the day, the spirit's watch and reason's workmaster. Farewell.

Two of the Clock

It is now the second hour and the point of the dial hath stepped over the first stroke, and now time begins to draw back the curtain of the night: the cock again calls to his hen, and the watch begin to bustle toward their discharge: the bell-man hath made a great part of his walk, and the nurse begins to huggle the child. . . the cat sits playing with the mouse which she hath catched, and the dog with his barking wakes the servants of the house: the studious now are near upon waking, and the thief will be gone, for fear of being taken: the foresters now be about their walks, and yet stealers sometime cozen the keepers: warreners now begin to draw homeward, and far dwellers from the town will be on the way to the market: the soldier now looks towards the *cour de garde*, and the corporal takes care for the relief of the watch: the earnest scholar will be now at his book, and the thrifty husbandman will rouse towards his rising: the seaman will now look out for light, and if the wind be fair, he calls for a can of beer: the fishermen now take the benefit of the tide, and he that bobs for eels will not be without worms. In sum, I hold it much of the nature of the first hour, but somewhat better. And to conclude, I think it the enemy of sleep and the entrance to exercise. Farewell.

Three of the Clock

It is now the third hour, and the windows of heaven begin to open, and the sun begins to colour the clouds in the sky, before he shew his face to the world: now are the spirits of life, as it were, risen out of death: the cock calls the servants to their day's work, and the grass horses are fetched from the pastures: the milk-maids begin to look toward their dairy, and the good housewife begins to look about the house: the porridge pot is on for the servants' breakfast, and hungry stomachs will soon be ready for their victual: the sparrow begins to chirp about the house, and the birds in the bushes will bid them welcome to the field: the shepherd sets on his pitch on the fire, and fills his tarpot ready for his flock: the wheel and the reel begin to be set ready, and a merry song makes the work seem easy: the ploughman falls to harness his horses, and the thresher begins to look toward the barn: the scholar that loves learning will be hard at his book, and the labourer by great will be walking toward his work. In brief it is a parcel of time to good purpose, the exercise of nature and the entrance into art. Farewell.

Four of the Clock

It is now the fourth hour, and the sun begins to send her beams abroad, whose glimmering brightness no eye can behold: now crows the cock lustily and claps his wings for joy of the light, and with his hens leaps lightly from his roost: now are the horses at their chaff and provender, the servants at breakfast, the milk-maid gone to the field, and the spinner at the wheel; and the shepherd with his dog are going toward the fold: now the beggars rouse them out of the hedges, and begin their morning craft; but if the constable come, beware the stocks: the birds now begin to flock, and the sparhawk begins to prey for his aerie: the thresher begins to stretch his long arms, and the thriving labourer will fall hard to his work: the quick-witted brain will be quoting of places, and the cunning workman will be trying of his skill: the hounds begin to be coupled for the chase, and the spaniels follow the falconer to the field: travellers begin to look toward the stable, where an honest hostler is worthy his reward.... In sum, I thus conclude of it: I hold it the messenger of action and the watch of reason. Farewell.

Five of the Clock

It is now five of the clock, and the sun is going apace upon his journey; and fie sluggards who would be asleep: the bells ring to prayer, and the streets are full of people, and the highways are stored with travellers: the scholars are up and going to school, and the rods are ready for the truants' correction: the maids are at milking, and the servants at plough, and the wheel goes merrily, while the mistress is by: the capons and the chickens must be served without door, and the hogs cry till they have their swill: the shepherd is almost gotten to his fold, and the herd begins to blow his horn through the town... the traveller now is well on his way, and if the weather be fair, he walks with the better cheer: the carter merrily whistles to his horse, and the boy with his sling casts stones at the crows.... In brief, not to stay too long upon it, I hold it the necessity of labour and the note of profit. Farewell.

Six of the Clock

It is now the sixth hour, the sweet time of the morning, and the sun at every window calls the sleepers from their beds: the marigold begins to open her leaves, and the dew on the ground doth sweeten the air: the falconers now meet with many a fair flight, and the hare and the hounds have made the huntsman good sport: the shops in the city begin to shew their wares, and the market people have taken their places: the scholars now have their forms, and whosoever cannot say his lesson must presently look for absolution: the forester now is drawing home to his lodge, and if his deer be gone, he may draw after cold scent: now begins the curst mistress to put her girls to their tasks, and a lazy hilding will do hurt among good workers: now the mower falls to whetting of his scythe, and the beaters of hemp give a ho! to every blow. . . . In sum, not to be tedious, I hold it the sluggard's shame and the labourer's praise. Farewell.

Seven of the Clock

It is now the seventh hour, and time begins to set the world hard to work; the milk-maids in their dairy to their butter and their cheese, the ploughmen to their ploughs and their barrows in the field, the scholars to their lessons, the lawyers to their cases, the merchants to their accounts, the shop-men to "What lack you?" and every trade to his business. Oh 'tis a world to see how life leaps about the limbs of the healthful: none but finds something to do: the wise to study, the strong to labour, the fantastic to make love, the poet to make verses, the player to con his part, and the musician to try his note: every one in his quality and according to his condition, sets himself to some exercise, either of the body or the mind: and therefore since it is a time of much labour and great use, I will thus briefly conclude of it: I hold it the enemy of idleness and employer of industry. Farewell.

Eight of the Clock

It is now the eighth hour, and good stomachs are ready for a breakfast: the huntsman now calls in his hounds, and at the fall of the deer the horns go apace: now begin the horses to breathe and the labourer to sweat, and, with quick hands, work rids apace... now the thresher begins to fall to his breakfast and eat apace, and work apace rids the corn quickly away: now the piper looks what he hath gotten since day, and the beggar, if he have hit well, will have a pot of the best: the traveller now begins to water his horse, and, if he were early up, perhaps a bait will do well. The ostler now makes clean his stables, and, if guests come in, he is not without his welcome. In conclusion, for all I find in it, I hold it the mind's travail and the body's toil. Farewell.

Nine of the Clock

It is now the ninth hour, and the sun is gotten up well toward his height, and the sweating traveller begins to feel the burden of his way: the scholar now falls to conning of his lesson, and the lawyer at the bar falls to pleading of his case... the market now grows to be full of people, and the shopmen now are in the heat of the market: the falconers now find it too hot flying, and the huntsmen begin to grow weary of their sport: the birders now take in their nets and their rods, and the fishermen send their fish to the market: the tavern and the ale-house are almost full of guests, and Westminster and Guild Hall are not without a word or two on both sides: the carriers now are loading out of town, and not a letter but must be paid for ere it pass: the crier now tries the strength of his throat, and the bearward leads his bear home after his challenge: the players' bills are almost all set up, and the clerk of the market begins to shew his office. In sum, in this hour there is much to do, as well in the city, as the country: and therefore to be short, I will thus make my conclusion: I hold it the toil of wit and the trial of reason. Farewell.

Ten of the Clock

It is now the tenth hour, and now preparation is to be made for dinner: the trenchers must be scraped and the napkins folded, the salt covered and the knives scoured and the cloth laid, the stools set ready and all for the table: there must be haste in the kitchen for the boiled and the roast, provision in the cellar for wine, ale and beer: the pantler and the butler must be ready in their office, and the usher of the hall must marshal the serving-men: the hawk must be set on the perch, and the dogs put into the kennel, and the guests that come to dinner must be invited against the hour: the scholars now fall to construe and parse, and the lawyer makes his client either a man or a mouse: the chapmen now draw home to their inns, and the shopmen fall to folding up their wares: the ploughman now begins to grow towards home, and the dairy maid, after her work, falls to cleansing of her vessels: the cook is cutting sops for broth, and the butler is chipping of loaves for the table: the minstrels begin to go towards the taverns, and the cursed crew visit the vile places. In sum, I thus conclude of it: I hold it the messenger to the stomach and the spirit's recreation. Farewell.

Eleven of the Clock

It is now the eleventh hour, children must break up school, lawyers must make home to their houses, merchants to the exchange, and gallants to the ordinary: the dishes set ready for the meat, and the glasses half full of fair water: now the market people make towards their horses, and the beggars begin to draw near the towns: the porridge, put off the fire, is set a cooling for the plough folk, and the great loaf and the cheese are set ready on the table: colleges and halls ring to dinner, and a scholar's commons is soon digested: the rich man's guests are at curtsy, and "I thank you": and the poor man's feast is "Welcome, and God be with you": the page is ready with his knife and his trencher, and the meat will be half cold, ere the guests can agree on their places: the cook voids the kitchen, and the butler the buttery, and the serving-men stand all ready at the dresser: the children are called to say grace before dinner, and the nice people rather look than eat: the gates be locked for fear of the beggars, and the minstrels called in to be ready with their music: the pleasant wit is now breaking a jest, and the hungry man puts his jaws to their proof. In sum, to conclude my opinion of it, I hold it the epicure's joy and the labourer's ease. Farewell.

Twelve of the Clock

It is now the twelfth hour, the sun is at his height, and the middle of the day: the first course is served in, and the second ready to follow: the dishes have been read over, and the reversion set by: the wine begins to be called for, and who waits not is chidden: talk passeth away time, and when stomachs are full discourses grow dull and heavy, but after fruit and cheese say grace and take away: now the markets are done, the exchange broke up, and the lawyers at dinner, and Duke Humphrey's servants make their walks in Paul's: the shopmen keep their shops, and their servants go to dinner: the traveller begins to call for a reckoning, and goes into the stable to see his horse eat his provender: the ploughman now is at the bottom of his dish, and the labourer draws out his dinner out of his bag: the beasts of the field take rest after their feed, and the birds of the air are at juke in the bushes: the lamb lies sucking while the ewe chews the cud, and the rabbit will scarce peep out of her burrow: the hare sits close asleep in her muse, while the dogs sit waiting for a bone from the trencher. In brief, for all I find of it, I thus conclude in it: I hold it the stomach's pleasure and the spirit's weariness. Farewell.

Midnight

Now is the sun withdrawn into his bedchamber, the windows of heaven are shut up, and silence with darkness have made a walk over the whole earth, and time is tasked to work upon the worst actions: yet virtue being herself, is never weary of well doing, while the best spirits are studying for the body's rest: dreams and visions are the haunters of troubled spirits, while nature is most comforted in the hope of the morning: the body now lies as a dead lump, while sleep, the pride of ease, lulls the senses of the slothful: the tired limbs now cease from their labours, and the studious brains give over their business: the bed is now an image of the grave, and the prayer of the faithful makes the pathway to Heaven . . . he that trusteth in God will be safe from the Devil. Farewell.

The Conclusion

And thus to conclude, for that it grows late, and a nod or two with an heavy eye makes me fear to prove a plain noddy, entreating your patience till to-morrow, and hoping you will censure mildly of this my fantastic labour, wishing I may hereafter please your senses with a better subject than this: I will in the mean time pray for your prosperity, and end with the English phrase, "God give you good night."

NICHOLAS BRETON, *Fantastickes*, 1626

Be cheerful, sir:
Our revels now are ended. These our actors,
As I foretold you, were all spirits and
Are melted into air, into thin air:
And, like the baseless fabric of this vision,
The cloud-capp'd towers, the gorgeous palaces,
The solemn temples, the great globe itself,
Yea, all which it inherit, shall dissolve
And, like this insubstantial pageant faded,
Leave not a rack behind. We are such stuff
As dreams are made on, and our little life
Is rounded with a sleep.

The Tempest, IV. i. 147–158

GLOSSARY

ADMIRATION. Astonishment.
ANGEL. Gold coin, about 10*s*.
ANTIC. Buffoon, grotesque pageant.
ANTIC-WOVEN. Fancifully embroidered.
ARGENT. Money, silver.
ARIFY. To dry up.
ARTIFICIAL. Skilful.
AVOID. To turn out, empty or clear away.
AVOIDANCE. Draining.
BABY-CAPS. ? Toy-caps.
BAIT. Food for a horse.
BARM. Yeast.
BETHLEHEM. I.e. the asylum of St Mary of Bethlehem, now called Bedlam.
BILL. List, note, advertisement.
BLUE-COATS. I.e. servants.
BOB. To fish with worms.
BORDERS. Plaits or braids of hair worn round the forehead or temples.
BOSSED. Puffed out, studded.
BRIDEWELL. A house of correction for women.
BRITTANY. I.e. Britain.
BROKER. I.e. pawnbroker.
BROW-BEATEN. Frowned at.
BUDGET. Leathern bag.
BUSH. I.e. ivy bush outside a tavern. A bunch or tuft of hair.
BUSKINS. Boots.
CAP-CASE. Bag or wallet.
CARTED. I.e. exposed like a criminal to public ignominy.
CATERPILLARS. I.e. brokers, extortioners.
CENSURE. To judge, think.
CHALLENGE. Claim.
CHAMBERLAIN. Male servant of an inn, in charge of the bedrooms.
CHARGE. "Great charge" = much money.
CHEAPEN. To buy, bargain for.
CHIRURGERY. Surgery.
CLAUSE. Conclusion.
CLEDGY. Cledge = clay.

Close. Private.
Closely. Secretly.
Coffin. Pie-dish.
Commorant. Resident.
Complexion. Humour, disposition.
Conditions. Constitution of body.
Consort. A band of musicians, choir.
Cony. Rabbit.
Cot-house. Shelter, shed.
Counterfeit crank. A rogue who feigns illness or disease.
Counter-tenor. Male alto voice.
Countervail. Counterbalance.
Cozen. Substantive = a dupe. Verb = to cheat.
Crab. Apple.
Crisped. Curled.
Cullis. Meat broth.
Cup-shotten. Intoxicated.
Curst. Shrewish.
Duke Humphrey's servants. Poor gallants who could not afford to dine, and so spent the dinner-hour loitering near Duke Humphrey's monument in St Paul's Walk.
Eftsoons. Soon.
Elf. Tangle.
Face-physic. Cosmetics.
Factors. Agents, assistants.
False gallop. Canter.
Farced. Pompous.
Feat. Trick, deed of skill.
Fisting-hound. Lap-dog.
Fleer. Grin, mock.
Flews. Large hanging chaps.
Forgetive. Inventive.
Forked heads. Arrow-heads.
Fray. To frighten.
Furcifer. Gallows-bird. Literally = fork-bearer.
Fustian. Coarse cloth.
Galliard. A lively dance.
Gallyslops. Loose breeches.
Geason. Rare.
Gulled. Full of ruts, worn away.
Gulling. Swallowing.

HEADBOROUGH. Parish officer, petty constable.
HENT. To take.
HILDING. Menial, servant.
HISTORIES. Plays, stories.
HOOKER. See p. 44.
HUKE. Cape, hooded cloak.
HUMOUR. Moistures of the body of any kind. Oddities of mind and disposition.
INTERMISSION. Play-time, interval.
JERK. Stroke, blow. Verb = to beat.
JET. Walk pompously.
JEW'S TRUMP. Jew's harp.
JOINED-BED. Bedstead (made by a joiner), considered a luxury at this period.
JOURNEY-MAN. Hired workman, one who has ceased to be a prentice but has not become a master-craftsman.
JUKE. "At juke (or jack) together" = chirping or clucking to each other.
JUMP. Exactly.
KEEL. To stir or cool (a pot on the fire).
KNOTS. Designs.
LAUNDER. Washerwoman.
LET. Verb = to hesitate, prevent. Substantive = hindrance.
LIBERTIES. The boundaries of the city.
LIGHTLY. I.e. as a general rule.
LOCKRAM. Coarse linen stuff.
LODGED. Checked for a while.
LORD OF MISRULE. Person in charge of Christmas festivities in a great man's house.
LUNEBURG TABLE. Lüneburg was a town in Hanover. In one of its churches there stood a table of gold from which, according to legend, a queen of England had had her crown made.
MALTWORM. A tippler.
MANURED. Cultivated, tilled, handled.
MEAN. Middle voice part in music, alto or tenor.
MEASURE. Dance.
MEWL. To mew like a cat, whimper.
MURRAIN. Plague.
MUSE. Hole in the hedge.
NICE. Fastidious.
NUNCHEON. Snack taken between meals, generally at noon.
OCCUPY. To traffic in, cultivate.

ORANGE-PILLS. Orange peel.
ORDINARY. Eating house. Public feast.
PACKS. Evil confederacies.
PAETUM. A corruption of the Brazilian *petum*=tobacco.
PARCEL-GILT. Partly gilded.
PAY. To chastise.
PEEVISH. Stubborn.
PEISE. To poise, weigh.
PELTING. Petty.
PICK. To knock down. To pitch.
PITCH. P. 38. Aim (an expression derived from falconry).
PLACES (quoting of). Making notes of passages he has read.
PLAYERS' BILLS. Placards announcing the play for the day.
PLEASANT. Jocose.
POINTED. Tied.
POINTS. Laces used (instead of buttons) to tie the lower to the upper garments.
PORTINGAL. Portuguese.
POTABLE. Drinkable.
POUNCE. To powder with cosmetics.
POXES. Skin diseases.
PRICK. A dot or mark.
PROCTOR. One who held a licence to collect alms for "spital-houses".
PROOF. Result.
PUKE. To vomit.
PURGATION. Examination.
QUALITY. Profession.
QUERN. Mill.
RACE. Root.
RADDLES. Laths.
RAISINS O' THE SUN. Dried grapes.
REAR-BANQUET. Collation taken after supper or dinner.
REVERSION. Scraps left over, remnant.
RID. To dispatch, clear away.
RING. Suspended from a post for riders to tilt at.
ROARER or roaring boy. A cant name for a swaggering bully.
ROGUES. *Rufflers*: see p. 42. *Uprightmen*: the highest rank of rogues. *Hookers*: see p. 44. *Rogues*: beggars pretending to seek kinsmen. *Wild rogues*: those born rogues. *Priggers of prancers*: horse-stealers. *Palliards*: beggars in patched cloaks. *Fraters*: pretended proctors (q.v.) with false licences. *Abrams*: see p. 41. *Freshwater mariners*:

pretended shipwrecked sailors. *Dummerers*: beggars pretending dumbness. *Drunken tinkers*: thieves posing as tinkers. *Swaddlers*: pedlars. *Jarkmen*: clerkly rogues who make false marriage licences and unite their comrades in wedlock. *Demanders for glimmer*: female beggars pretending to have lost all that they had by fire. *Bawdy-baskets*: female pedlars. *Morts*: female beggars not legally married. *Autem morts*: legally married female rogues. *Doxies*: mistresses to rogues. *Dells*: maiden beggars. *Kinching morts*: young female rogues. *Kinching coes*: young male rogues.

SANDED. Sandy-coloured.

SCANT. Scarcely.

SERGEANT. Police officer.

SHIFT. To avoid.

SHIFTING. Deceitful, shifty.

SHOEING THE WILD MARE. Some Christmas game, now forgotten.

SLIPPER-MERCHANTS. Slippery customers.

SNORT. To snore.

SNUFF. To inhale. "To take in snuff" = to take offence.

SPENDING. P. 10. Utterance.

STALL. Bench before a shop.

STARK. Stiff.

STAULING-KEN. A house that will receive stolen goods.

STILL. Always, ever.

STOVES. Houses or rooms for hot vapour baths.

SWAG-BELLIED. With a large overhanging belly.

TAKE UP A QUARREL. To settle a quarrel.

TARLTON (Richard) died 1588. A famous Elizabethan comic actor, said to be the original of Yorick in *Hamlet*.

TAWE OUT. To extort.

TISSUE. Cloth of gold.

TRICK. To deck out.

TROPE. Figure of speech.

TRUSS. Breeches. Verb = to tie up the "points" (q.v.).

UTTER. To deliver, speak.

VIZARD. Mask.

VOID. See AVOID.

WAITERS. Attendants.

WARDEN. A kind of pear.

WARRENER. Keeper of poultry and rabbits.

WATSHOD OR WATCHET. Pale blue colour.

WELT. Strip, border. Verb = to patch.

CAMBRIDGE: PRINTED BY
W. LEWIS, M.A.
AT THE UNIVERSITY PRESS